PYTHAGOREAN POLITICS IN SOUTHERN ITALY
An Analysis of the Sources

By KURT VON FRITZ

OCTAGON BOOKS

A DIVISION OF FARRAR, STRAUS AND GIROUX

New York   1977

Copyright 1940 by
Columbia University Press

Reprinted 1977
by special arrangement with Columbia University Press

OCTAGON BOOKS
A DIVISION OF FARRAR, STRAUS & GIROUX, INC.
19 Union Square West
New York, N.Y. 10003

Library of Congress Cataloging in Publication Data

Fritz, Kurt von, 1900-
    Pythagorean politics in southern Italy.

        Reprint of the ed. published by Columbia University Press, New York.
        Includes index.
        1. Pythagoras and Pythagorean school. 2. Aristoxenus. 3. Diaearchus, of Messene. 4. Timaeus, of Tauromenium. I. Title.
B199.F7   1977   182′.2   77-2843
ISBN 0-374-92939-4

Printed in USA by
Thomson-Shore, Inc.
Dexter, Michigan

PYTHAGOREAN POLITICS
IN SOUTHERN ITALY

PREFACE

THE HISTORY of the political activities of the Pythagoreans in Southern Italy from the end of the sixth to the beginning of the fourth century B.C. presents an extremely interesting, but at the same time very difficult problem. For all the ancient tradition about the Pythagoreans is interwoven with legends, and only a very few political events that occurred in that region during the period in question are known independently of this very special tradition.

Lately some hope has arisen that new sources of information may be opened up by means of the most modern methods of inquiry. It is true that the excavations at Metapontum and Sybaris which have been undertaken during the last few years have not yet yielded any results from which reliable conclusions as to the history of the Pythagoreans can be drawn,[1] but U. Kahrstedt[2] in a very interesting paper—though he is perhaps a little overconfident in some of his more detailed

[1] Cf. E. Galli, "Metaponto," *Atti e Memorie della Società Magna Grecia*, 1927, and "Alla ricerca di Sibari," *ibid.*, 1929; also G. Bognani, *Archivio storico per la Calabria e la Lucania*, I, 261 ff. As to the supposed discoveries of Macchioro (Zagreus, Florence, 1930) concerning the Pythagoreans at Kroton and Sybaris, cf. Zanotti-Bianco, *Archivio storico per la Calabria e la Lucania*, II, 285, note 1.

[2] U. Kahrstedt, "Grossgriechenland im 5. Jahrhundert," *Hermes*, LIII (1932), 180 ff.; cf. G. Gianelli, *La Magna Grecia da Pitagora a Pirro* (Pubblicazioni della Università Cattolica del Sacro Cuore, IX). Gianelli tries to make use of Kahrstedt's results for the elaboration of a more complete history of Southern Italy; but a great many of his conclusions are, if not altogether improbable, at least highly conjectural.

reconstructions of the chronology—has proved beyond doubt that a careful examination of the coins of Kroton and of some other cities of Southern Italy enables us to trace, to some extent, the development of the interrelations of this centre of Pythagorean activities with other communities from the end of the sixth to the middle of the fifth century.

A good deal more may perhaps be expected from the future. For there are several problems, especially of chronology, that may be solved by further numismatic studies and the results of later excavations.

However, there are certain limitations to the usefulness of archeological evidence for a historical reconstruction of this kind. It may help to fix the dates of certain events or to determine the extent of Pythagorean rule or political influence in Southern Italy. But numismatic and archeological chronology itself depends on the knowledge of fixed dates from which the investigation may work forward and backward; and the knowledge of these dates is mostly derived from literary sources and is therefore dependent on the reliability of this kind of tradition. In this respect the analysis of the sources is a prerequisite and auxiliary to archeological investigation. In other respects it is still more important. In order to determine the character and political significance of an event which may be fixed chronologically through archeological and numismatic investigation one will always have to consult the literary tradition in the first place; and to the solution of the more comprehensive and far reaching questions, as for instance concerning the character of the Pythagorean "rule" and the possible changes which it underwent in the course of time, archeological evidence will scarcely ever contribute very much.

For all these reasons the literary tradition has not lost but gained in importance, now that new sources of information have already opened up and are likely to open up in a near future; and a new analysis seems very much needed. For though a number of excellent and highly constructive contributions towards the solution of the most important problems have been made during the last few decades, these problems are by no means solved; and in many cases the authors of those contributions have arrived at widely differing results. This is largely due to the fact that they have not always distinguished carefully enough between those of their results which can be considered as fairly certain and those which at most can lay claim to a higher or lower degree of probability. It will therefore be my chief aim to avoid this mistake. For, especially with a view to later discoveries, it seems to me more useful to determine with certainty, for instance, within which limits a certain event must be dated rather than to make the attempt to arrive at an exact date on the basis of insufficient evidence and through uncertain constructions.

It is in the nature of an inquiry of this kind that it is largely critical and that not everything that will be said is absolutely new. In one case—in the reconstruction of Timaios' version—it has been necessary to put the whole material, mostly collected by other scholars, before the reader, for since it is scattered in a great many different modern contributions, a mere reference to them would not have been sufficient to give a full insight into the nature of the evidence. I have also repeated some of the excellent observations of A. Delatte concerning the character of Aristoxenos' sources since they are extremely important for the further investigation. In all other cases however I have merely given the bibliographical reference whenever it seemed to me that a problem had been settled conclusively and to its full extent before this, and I have given a full quotation of the arguments of my predecessors only where I have arrived at different results.[3]

[3] I did not indicate where my results happen either to coincide with or to deviate from the accounts given of this epoch in the numerous

But I make use of this occasion to acknowledge my great indebtedness especially to the works of A. Delatte and A. Rostagni, without whose penetrating investigations the present book could not have been written. I am also greatly indebted to Mrs. Alexander Baldwin Brett of the American Numismatic Society, who has been so kind as to discuss the numismatical evidence with me and to answer my many questions in a field in which she is one of the foremost experts.

It is perhaps necessary to say a few words concerning the division of this book into chapters. Since all the problems are closely connected it was not possible to deal with each problem in a separate chapter. Since Iamblichos and Porphyrios did not use Aristoxenos directly but through the medium of the works of Neanthes and Nikomachos, it was necessary to link up the reconstruction of Aristoxenos with a reconstruction of the share of these authors in later tradition. For the same reason the reconstruction of Timaios' version had to be connected with a discussion of the work of Apollonios. Since in one case it had been doubtful whether a fragment belonged to Aristoxenos or to Dikaiarchos, these two authors, though both of them are "primary authorities," had to be discussed in the same chapter. Some chronological questions had to be discussed in the chapter on Timaios since their solution is contributory to the reconstruction of his version, while the general chronology naturally could not be discussed until the analysis of the sources had been completed. In spite of these difficulties I hope that I have avoided unnecessary repetitions.

In conclusion I may perhaps be allowed to make a few remarks concerning the results of this investigation. As far as

---

modern works on Greek history or Southern Italian history in general, except in the few cases in which these works contain an explicit discussion of the sources. It would have been quite impossible to draw a line between the works to be included and those to be excluded; to include all of them would have increased the number and extent of the notes beyond all measure without any real advantage to the reader.

PREFACE

the chronology is concerned it is in the nature of things that they are only preliminary and a starting point for future investigations. In the attempt to determine the character of the Pythagorean "rule" I have at least tried to arrive at somewhat more final conclusions. If this attempt has been successful, it may perhaps throw some new light on the complicated and much discussed question of interrelations between early Pythagoreanism and Platonism. But the analysis of the sources may perhaps also claim some interest of its own. For the tradition about the political history of the early Pythagoreans presents an outstanding example of reinterpretation of historical events under the influence of political tendencies during the earlier period, and under the influence of literary tendencies during the later period of the tradition.

Finally, I wish to thank my colleague, Professor Clinton W. Keyes, for his kind help in correcting my not yet always faultless English and Columbia University Press not only for publishing this book but also for the great care with which the details of the work were handled.

KURT VON FRITZ

Columbia University in the
City of New York

CONTENTS

	Preface	v
I.	Reconstruction of the Versions of Aristoxenos and Dikaiarchos	3
II.	The Sources of Dikaiarchos and Aristoxenos and the Reliability of Their Accounts	27
III.	Reconstruction of Timaios' Version and the Reliability of His Accounts	33
IV.	The Chronological Questions and the Numismatic Evidence	68
V.	The Character of the "Pythagorean Rule" in Southern Italy	94
	Appendix	103
	General Index	109

PYTHAGOREAN POLITICS
IN SOUTHERN ITALY

CHAPTER I

Reconstruction of the Versions of Aristoxenos and Dikaiarchos

SINCE of the scholars who have treated it[1] Corssen has dealt most thoroughly, though perhaps not most successfully, with the problem of the reconstruction of Aristoxenos' share in the later tradition on the political history of the Pythagoreans the present inquiry may perhaps for some time follow his lead.

Corssen begins his study with an attempt to determine the share of Neanthes of Kyzikos in the accounts given by Porphyrios, Iamblichos, and Diogenes Laertios in their biographies of Pythagoras.

Porphyrios[2] states that a noble Krotonian of the name of Kylon approached Pythagoras with the request to be ad-

[1] Important studies in the questions discussed in this chapter are: E. Rohde, "Die Quellen des Iamblichus in seiner Biographie des Pythagoras," *Kleine Schriften*, I, 102–172; G. F. Unger, "Zur Geschichte der Pythagoreer," *Sitz.-Berichte d. Muench. Akad. phil.-hist. Klasse*, 1883, 140–192; J. Mewaldt, *De Aristoxeni Pythagoricis sententiis et vita Pythagorica* (Dissert., Berlin, 1904); W. Bertermann, *De Iamblichi vitae Pythagoricae fontibus* (Dissert., Koenigsberg, 1913); F. Corssen, "Die Sprengung des pythagoreischen Bundes," *Philologus*, LXXI, 332 ff.; A. Delatte, "Essai sur la politique pythagoricienne III: Les Luttes politiques," *Bibliothèque de la Faculté de Liége*, XXIX, 203 ff.

[2] *Vit. Pyth.* 54.

mitted to the Pythagorean order. When his request was refused he stirred up a rebellion against Pythagoras and his followers in the course of which most of the Pythagoreans were burnt to death in the house of the famous athlete Milon at Kroton or stoned to death while trying to escape. But, says Porphyrios, according to the opinion of some other authors all this happened in the absence of Pythagoras himself, since, at that time, he had gone to Delos in order to care for his former teacher Pherekydes who suffered from φθειρίασις. In this account Neanthes is quoted only for the supplementary remark that Archippos and Lysis were the only ones to escape from the burning building, and that Lysis went later to Greece where he became the teacher of Epaminondas.

In 56 Porphyrios goes on to say that Dikaiarchos καὶ οἱ ἀκριβέστεροι contend that Pythagoras was present at the time of the catastrophe, since Pherekydes died at a much earlier date. There follows a lengthy account of Pythagoras' escape and of the further vicissitudes of his life up to his death, and, in addition, a rather gruesome story of how the Pythagoreans sacrificed their own lives in order to save their master.

Following this, the question is discussed: how could the philosophy of the Pythagoreans have survived, though there existed no literary documents? Corssen contends that this latest part of the account[3] is a continuation of the story told in Sections 54 and 55 and that both parts are taken from Neanthes.

His arguments are the following: (1) The names of Lysis and Archippos that had been mentioned in the quotation from Neanthes[4] recur towards the end of Porphyrios 57. (2) The discussion in Section 57 of the way in which the Pythagorean doctrine was preserved and handed down to posterity after the disaster is very similar to the discussion of

[3] Porph. 57, ii-58.
[4] Porph. 55.

the same subject attributed to Neanthes by Diogenes Laertios.[5] (3) A rare use of the word θηρᾶν to design a mental, not a physical, activity is found in Porphyrios 54 as well as in Section 57. This suggests that not only Sections 57, ii–58 and 55 but also Section 54 can be traced to Neanthes, though he is quoted directly only for a supplementary remark in Porphyrios, Section 55.

These are undoubtedly very strong arguments, and it will be seen later that Corssen's conclusion is confirmed by further evidence.

The second question which Corssen tries to answer concerns the extent to which Dikaiarchos is a source for the passage in Porphyrios. He points out that the whole passage from Δικαίαρχος καὶ οἱ ἀκριβέστεροι in Section 56 to οἱ δέ φασιν in Section 57 must be taken from Dikaiarchos since its last sentence ἐν δὲ τῇ περὶ Μεταπόντιον κτλ. is quoted as Dikaiarchean by Diogenes Laertios VIII, 40. In this respect too Corssen is undoubtedly right.

At this point Aristoxenos comes in. The passage taken from Dikaiarchos begins with the words [Δικαίαρχός φησι] παρεῖναι αὐτὸν τῇ ἐπιβουλῇ. Φερεκύδην γὰρ πρὸ τῆς ἐκ Σάμου ἀπάρσεως τελευτῆσαι κτλ. Corssen contends that this is a criticism directed against some other ancient author and that this other author must be Aristoxenos. Since the question whether this contention is to be accepted or rejected is a crucial point in the whole problem, it must be examined very carefully.

Here, too, Corssen has three arguments: (1) In the context the criticism seems directed against Neanthes. Since, however, in Corssen's opinion Neanthes lived much later than Dikaiarchos, it must originally have been directed against an earlier author. This author must have been Aristoxenos because he was a contemporary of Dikaiarchos and the first to write a Βίος Πυθαγόρου. (2) Confirmation of this conclusion can be

[5] VIII, 55.

found in the fact that Aristoxenos is quoted by Diogenes Laertios[6] as mentioning the sojourn of Pythagoras with Pherekydes on Delos, though in this quotation no reference whatever is made to the date of this event. (3) Dikaiarchos in his criticism uses the same word ἄπαρσις which is also used in a quotation from Aristoxenos.[7] This seems to indicate that Dikaiarchos used the very words of the author whose opinion he tried to refute.

Let us examine each of these arguments. (1) As to the contention that Dikaiarchos cannot have criticized Neanthes for chronological reasons, one might object that the earlier of the two Neanthes of Kyzikos, who was, in all likelihood, the author of the Βίος Πυθαγόρου, was only about 25 years younger than Dikaiarchos. A priori, therefore, it would not be entirely impossible to assume that Dikaiarchos' criticism was directed against Neanthes himself. But this is excluded by some other observations. Delatte[8] has shown by a comparison of Porphyrios 54 with a quotation from Aristoxenos in Iamblichos 248 that Neanthes must have taken the first part of his account from Aristoxenos. By a combination of Diogenes Laertios VIII, 2 and Porphyrios 1, where Kleanthes (i.e., Neanthes)[9] is quoted, he has also proved that Neanthes did not share the belief that Pythagoras was at Delos at the time of the disaster. This makes the assumption impossible that Dikaiarchos' criticism was directed against Neanthes. Thus far, therefore, the first argument of Corssen seems to be strengthened. Dikaiarchos' criticism must be directed against an author earlier than Neanthes and used by him. In addition, Neanthes has notoriously made use of Aristoxenos.

[6] I, 11, 118.
[7] Porph. 9.
[8] *Musée belge*, XII, 205 ff.
[9] Cf. F. Jacoby, *Die Fragmente der griechischen Historiker*, II, 84 F 29, and commentary.

But Delatte's discovery makes it necessary to examine the whole question again.

If Neanthes did not share the opinion that Pythagoras was at Delos when the disaster occurred and yet—as we see in Porphyrios 55—quoted this opinion, he must have mentioned his own opinion also and in all likelihood supported it by the quotation of other authorities. This he obviously did by calling upon Δικαίαρχος καὶ οἱ ἀκριβέστεροι. In this case the quotation of οἱ μέν as well as that from Dikaiarchos which is put in contrast with it must be taken from Neanthes; that is, not only Sections 54-55 and 57, ii-58, as Corssen discovered, belong to the same extract from the work of Neanthes, but Section 56 also.

This gives a new starting point to the inquiry. The first part of Neanthes' account—as far as it is reproduced by Porphyrios, for he gives only an abstract—is taken from Aristoxenos. Then he arrives at a controversial question. He quotes two opposite opinions, one represented by οἱ μέν, the other by Δικαίαρχος καὶ οἱ ἀκριβέστεροι. Are οἱ μέν identical with Aristoxenos?

There is certainly no historical necessity to make this assumption. For though Aristoxenos was the first to write a Βίος Πυθαγόρου proper, many Pythagorean legends had been told, for instance by Herakleides Pontikos in various of his dialogues. That Neanthes, who lived not so very much later than Dikaiarchos, considered other traditions as well is shown by the words καὶ οἱ ἀκριβέστεροι. That oral tradition was also discussed is proved by the remark of Dikaiarchos: ἐγένοντο μεγάλαι στάσεις ἃς ἔτι καὶ νῦν οἱ περὶ τοὺς τόπους μ ν η μ ο - ν ε ύ ο ν τ α ι καὶ δ ι η γ ο ῦ ν τ α ι.[10] It is therefore not necessary to assume that it was Aristoxenos whom Dikaiarchos wanted to refute.

As to Neanthes' way of quoting there is no reason either

[10] Porph. 56.

why one should assume that with οἱ μὲν he is still referring to Aristoxenos, since he obviously makes a fresh start. One might even wonder why he should have said οἱ μὲν instead of Ἀριστόξενος if, having followed Aristoxenos thus far, he wished to indicate that in this special question he could not agree with him. Thus far then, there is still a slight possibility that οἱ μὲν include Aristoxenos, but this is certainly not proved by Corssen's first argument.

(2) His second argument can only be used in support of the first one and has no strength by itself. For the question is not whether Aristoxenos mentioned Pythagoras' sojourn at Delos or not, but how he dated it. Apart from this the wording of the quotation from Aristoxenos in Diogenes Laertios I, 11, 118 is entirely different from that of the οἱ μὲν quotation in the passage from Neanthes. This is all the more remarkable because in all the other cases in which the same author is quoted for the same story a good deal of the wording is also the same though there are usually a few slighter differences, because the original is shortened in different ways.

There is, however, another passage—in Porphyrios 15—the wording of which is much more similar to that of the quotation from Aristoxenos in Diogenes Laertios I, 11, 118,[11] and this passage says that Pythagoras returned to Samos after having buried his master at Delos; that is, it dates the sojourn at Delos in the time before Pythagoras' migration to Italy. In addition, this passage is followed—after a short interruption on Milon's training as an athlete—by the words: Μετὰ δὲ ταῦτα τῆς Πολυκράτους τυραννίδος Σαμίους καταλαβούσης, οὐ πρέπον ἡγούμενος ὁ Πυθαγόρας, ἐν τοιαύτῃ πολιτείᾳ βιοῦν ἀνδρὶ φιλοσόφῳ διενοήθη εἰς Ἰταλίαν ἀ π α ί ρ ε ι ν.[12] This is the same statement as that attributed to Aristoxenos

---
[11] In order to make the comparison easy I juxtapose the three passages: see Parallel I.
[12] Porph. 16.

Parallel I

Porphyrios 15

Νοσήσαντα δὲ τὸν Φερεκύδην ἐν Δήλῳ θεραπεύσας καὶ ἀποθανόντα θάψας εἰς Σάμον ἐπανῆλθε πόθῳ τοῦ συγγενέσθαι Ἑρμοδάμαντι τῷ Κρεωφυλίῳ

Diogenes Laertios I, 118

Ἀριστόξενος δ' ἐν τῷ περὶ Πυθαγόρου καὶ τῶν γνωρίμων αὐτοῦ φησι ν ο σ ή σ α ν τ α αὐτόν (sc. τὸν Φερεκύδην) ὑπὸ Πυθαγόρου τ α φ ῆ ν α ι. οἱ δὲ (not Aristoxenos) φθειριάσαντα τὸν βίον τελευτῆναι.

Porphyrios 55 (οἱ μὲν)

Ὡς γὰρ Φερεκύδην τὸν Σύριον αὐτοῦ διδάσκαλον γενόμενον εἰς Δῆλον ἐπεπόρευτο νοσοκομήσων αὐτὸν περιπετῆ γενόμενον τῷ ἱστορουμένῳ τῆς φθειριάσεως πάθει.

by Porphyrios 9, and here again recurs the word which Corssen himself considers characteristic of Aristoxenos. It would be a very strange coincidence indeed if this whole passage were not taken from Aristoxenos. But if this was the case, he dated Pythagoras' sojourn at Delos in the period before his migration to Italy.[13] He shared the opinion of Dikaiarchos in this respect,[14] and Dikaiarchos' criticism cannot be directed against him.

(3) It is scarcely worth while to refute Corssen's third argument. That Dikaiarchos used the same word ἄπαρσις as Aristoxenos is explained by the fact that he made use of the date given by Aristoxenos for Pythagoras' sojourn on Delos in order to refute the version of οἱ μέν. The use of the same word shows that he agreed with Aristoxenos in this point and used him, not that he wanted to refute him.[15]

It was necessary to establish this point very carefully. For apart from the gain of a few more fragments that can be ascribed to Aristoxenos with certainty, we shall see in the course of this inquiry that the decision of this little question has rather far-reaching consequences.

[13] The relation between Aristoxenos' version of this story and the one given by Diodoros X, 4 will be discussed later: see pp. 25 f.
[14] That, in spite of this, Neanthes did not say Ἀριστόξενος καὶ οἱ ἀκριβέστεροι but quoted Dikaiarchos instead can be easily explained by the fact that he is about to insert the version of Dikaiarchos, which, though agreeing with that of Aristoxenos in regard to the chronology of Pythagoras' stay at Delos, deviates from it in other respects.
[15] This is the only rational explanation of the coincidence; for Aristoxenos uses the word ἄπαρσις in connection with Pythagoras' migration to Italy. If then, as Corssen contends, he had dated the sojourn at Delos in the time of the disaster at Kroton, the whole story of the foundation and growth of the Pythagorean order would have had to be told between both events. How, then, can one assume that Dikaiarchos took over the word from the passage which he wanted to criticize, since Aristoxenos used it in an entirely different part of his work? Besides, a comparison of Porph. 22 (Aristoxenos) and Porph. 19 (Dikaiarchos) shows that Dikaiarchos made direct use of Aristoxenos in other places also.

ARISTOXENOS AND DIKAIARCHOS

Let us then turn to other passages in which Aristoxenos is quoted. Most important among them is Iamblichos 248-51. As an introduction we find here the rather amazing statement that all authorities agree that the Krotonian disaster occurred during the absence of Pythagoras. This is not only in open contradiction with the quotation from Dikaiarchos in Porphyrios 56 but to some extent even with the story which Iamblichos himself tells in the following chapters.

The following statement: Αἱ δὲ αἰτίαι τῆς ἐπιβουλῆς πλείονες λέγονται, μία μὲν ἀπὸ τῶν Κυλωνείων λεγομένων ἀνδρῶν τοιάδε γενομένη is, at first sight, scarcely less surprising, since all the ancient sources of which we know connect the event in some way with Kylon. Iamblichos himself, at any rate, does not mention any version differing from Sections 248-51 in this respect. All this shows how carelessly Iamblichos put together the pieces of information derived from other sources.

After this introduction Iamblichos gives an account of the history of the Pythagoreans from the last years of the life of Pythagoras to the final dissolution of the order. It runs as follows:

(1) Kylon, a rich and influential Krotonian, seeks admission to the Pythagorean order, but his request is denied by Pythagoras, who at that time is already a very old man.

(2) Then Kylon and his followers stir up enmity against Pythagoras and the Pythagoreans. For this reason Pythagoras goes to Metapontum, where he dies.

(3) This does not put an end to the enmity between the Pythagoreans and the Kylonians. The latter—it should be noticed that from now on Iamblichos speaks always of the Kylonians while in the preceding part of his account he had always spoken of αὐτὸς ὁ Κύλων καὶ οἱ μετ' ἐκείνου—continue to stir up trouble. But for some time (μέχρι τινός) the καλοκἀγαθία of the Pythagoreans prevails and the πόλεις—this indicates that some other cities in addition to Kroton are by now

under Pythagorean rule—prefer to be administered (οἰκονομεῖσθαι κατὰ τὰς πολιτείας) by them.

(4) Finally, however (τέλος δέ), the Kylonians go so far as to set fire to the house of the athlete Milon while the Pythagoreans hold a political meeting there and burn all of them to death except Archippos and Lysis, who, young and ablebodied, manage to escape.

In the third and fourth sections of this passage the use of the words διετέλουν, μέχρι τινός, τέλος δέ in three consecutive sentences indicates that this part of the account is meant to cover not too short a period, just as the word Κυλώνειοι indicates that from now on the author refers to events that occurred after the death of Kylon.

(5) Following the Krotonian catastrophe the Pythagoreans cease to take part in the administration of the cities (ἐπαύσαντο τῆς ἐπιμελείας) for two reasons: (a) because their leaders are dead, (b) because the cities seem not to take any interest in their fate and, at any rate, do not take any action.

This again seems to presuppose that the political leadership of the Pythagoreans was not confined to Kroton, since they obviously expected other cities to come to their aid and to punish their assailants. This is not at variance with the statement that all the Pythagorean leaders were killed at Kroton. For it is not necessary to assume that all of those who took part in the meeting at Kroton lived in this place. It is quite conceivable that many of them had come from other places for this special occasion.

On the other hand, it is left uncertain what obligations the other cities had towards the Pythagoreans. The Pythagoreans obviously were not their rulers in such a way that they had the decision over peace and war. Otherwise the author could hardly speak of a mere neglect (ὀλιγωρία) of these cities to help them. He leaves no doubt that the Pythagoreans wanted to help one another. If therefore they had been absolute rulers in Metapontum and other cities, a refusal to come to the rescue of the Pythagoreans at Kroton would have meant a revolution. But the author does not mention anything of the kind.

(6) Of the two men who escape from the catastrophe, Archippos goes to his native town Tarentum, while Lysis emigrates, first to Achaia and thence, after some time, to Thebes, where later he becomes the tutor and friend of Epaminondas and finally dies at a very old age.

(7) The following part of the account is confused in the manuscripts, where it runs as follows: οἱ δὲ λοιποὶ τῶν Πυθαγορείων ἀπέστησαν τῆς Ἰταλίας πλὴν Ἀρχύτου τοῦ Ταραντίνου. Ἀθροισθέντες εἰς τὸ Ῥήγιον ἐκεῖ διέτριβον μετ' ἀλλήλων. Προιόντος δὲ τοῦ χρόνου καὶ τῶν πολιτευμάτων ἐπὶ τὸ χεῖρον προβαινόντων σπουδαιότατοι δὲ ἦσαν Ἐχεκράτης κτλ. E. Rohde[16] was the first to see that this otherwise incomprehensible passage can be restored by a simple rearrangement and the omission of one δέ. The original context must have been: Οἱ δὲ λοιποὶ τῶν Πυθαγορείων ἀθροισθέντες εἰς τὸ Ῥήγιον ἐκεῖ διέτριβον μετ' ἀλλήλων. Προιόντος δὲ τοῦ χρόνου καὶ τῶν πολιτευμάτων ἐπὶ τὸ χεῖρον προβαινόντων ἀπέστησαν τῆς Ἰταλίας πλὴν Ἀρχύτου τοῦ Ταραντίνου. Σπουδαιότατοι δὲ κτλ.

If this emendation is accepted,[17] it becomes clear that two further stages of the historical development were distinguished by the author: (a) A short time after the catastrophe the Pythagoreans try to create a new centre of their activity at Rhegion, without, however—if the preceding remarks are to be taken seriously—making any further attempt to regain their political influence. (b) Later, in consequence of a further deterioration of the political situation, they leave Italy altogether.

(8) The passage ends with an enumeration of the σπουδαιό-

[16] *Kleine Schriften*, II, 114 note.
[17] See Appendix A.

τατοι among the last Pythagoreans, who tried to preserve the old customs and doctrines in exile while the school was gradually dying out. They are exactly the same as those mentioned by Diogenes Laertios[18] as personally known to Aristoxenos.

(9) There follows the sentence: Ταῦτα μὲν οὖν 'Αριστόξενος διηγεῖται. Νικόμαχος δὲ τὰ μὲν ἄλλα συνομολογεῖ τούτοις, παρὰ δὲ τὴν ἀποδημίαν τοῦ Πυθαγόρου φησὶ γεγονέναι τὴν ἐπιβουλὴν ταύτην. This sentence is still stranger than the introductory portion quoted above. For it seems to presuppose that according to the preceding account the disaster at Kroton occurred while Pythagoras was present, though this is not only not the case but the introduction says expressly that it happened in the absence of the master and that all authors agree on this point.

However this self-contradictory remark may have originated,[19] it illustrates again Iamblichos' carelessness in putting together the information derived from his sources, and it proves also that he did not use the authors whom he quotes directly but found the quotations in works of later origin.

Much more important, however, is the question as to whether the quotation of Aristoxenos in Section 251 refers to the whole passage, Sections 248–51, or only to part of it. The form of the quotation (Ταῦτα μὲν οὖν 'Αριστόξενος διηγεῖται), especially when taken with the fact that the same kind of quotation (Ταῦτα μὲν οὖν 'Αριστόξενος ἀπήγγειλε, φησὶν) in Iamblichos 237 as well as in Porphyrios 60 refers undoubtedly to the whole story preceding the quotation, suggests that the whole passage of Sections 248–51 is meant. Considering Iamblichos' notorious carelessness in quoting, however, this is not sufficient evidence.

In addition, Corssen[20] has tried to prove that the chapter

[18] VIII, 1, 46.
[19] See Appendix B.
[20] *Op. cit.*, pp. 340 ff.

is a mixture of different traditions which are partly at variance with one another and only artificially molded into one story. Let us therefore examine his arguments. (1) In his opinion the statement that the Pythagoreans left Italy altogether is so utterly at variance with the facts that it cannot be imputed to Aristoxenos. But we shall see later that, far from being unhistorical, this statement, if taken *cum grano salis* as any such general statement must be,[21] and if considered as referring to the time of Archytas[22] is confirmed by very substantial independent historical evidence. (2) Corssen further contends that the chapter contains several contradictory statements: (A) According to Iamblichos 249 the Pythagoreans who did not take part in the meeting at Kroton remained in Italy, but according to Section 251 the Pythagoreans left Italy altogether. (B) According to Section 249 one should assume that the order was completely destroyed, but according to Sections 250–251 they lost only their political influence. This difficulty disappears entirely through the transposition of words made by Rohde. For if this transposition is accepted as in fact it must,[23] it becomes quite clear that the seemingly contradictory statements refer to different epochs of Pythagorean history. (3) The main reason, how-

[21] It should not be necessary to point out that any historian who says that the Huguenots left France or that the Visigoths left Italy "altogether" does not imply that absolutely none of them remained. In the particular case in question the meaning is especially clear, since "leaving altogether" is here put into contrast with the attempt to create a new center of philosophical and religious, if not political, activity in Southern Italy. Apart from this it is rather curious that Corssen, who thinks that a statement which (if taken *cum grano salis*) is historically perfectly sound cannot be imputed to Aristoxenos, does not hesitate, in another place, to assume that Aristoxenos committed the egregious chronological error of dating the youth of Lysis, the teacher of Epaminondas, in the lifetime of Pythagoras.
[22] Cf. Appendix A.
[23] *Ibid.*

ever, why Corssen cannot accept the whole story as Aristoxenian is that it is irreconcilable with the assumption that the disaster at Kroton occurred at the time of Pythagoras' absence in Delos. But Corssen's opinion that this version was accepted by Aristoxenos has already been refuted. This disposes of his last argument.

At the same time the examination of Corssen's arguments has proved that the story told in Iamblichos 348–51 is entirely coherent, though the original has obviously been shortened. This is all the more significant since Iamblichos is notoriously incapable of making up a coherent story by himself. In addition, there is a passage in Section 349 pointing forward to the end of the whole story for which Aristoxenos is expressly quoted. This makes it extremely probable that the whole passage goes back to the work of Aristoxenos.

There is one more argument in favor of this assumption, an argument which will gain in weight in the course of this investigation. In all the passages of ancient authors in which Aristoxenos is quoted there is a marked tendency to represent the Pythagoreans as lovers of freedom and as the representatives of a liberal government. This tendency is also very noticeable throughout the whole passage of Iamblichos 248–51, especially if it is compared with other versions of the same story. Kylon is not a popular leader, as in other authors, but a rich debauchee, and his resentment is not caused by political grievances, but by private disappointment. The other Italian cities, with the exception of Kroton—and even in Kroton it is only the faction of Kylon that does so—do not rebel against Pythagorean rule, but merely neglect to help them. It seems that some cities ask the Pythagoreans to take a leading part in their administration and government, but the author avoids carefully any reference to the Pythagoreans as seeking political influence, much less as trying to become actual rulers. All this is in marked contrast to the account given by other ancient authors, as the second chapter of this investigation will show.

The other fragments of Aristoxenos' work on the Pythagoreans are shorter and do not cover such a long period. They can be discussed in chronological order.

(1) If it is safe to assume that Aristoxenos dated the death of Pherekydes in the period before Pythagoras' migration to Italy,[24] the sojourn on Delos is the first event mentioned in the fragments.[25]

(2) The similarity in the wording of the passage Diogenes Laertios I, 11, 118 and the passage Porphyrios 15 is so great that the latter has also to be attributed to Aristoxenos. But here the quotation extends a little further. Aristoxenos mentions that Pythagoras, having buried his teacher, returned to Samos in order to study with Hermodamas, a descendant of Kreophylos, the famous Homerid.

(3) The next fragment in chronological order is found in Porphyrios 9, where Aristoxenos is again quoted by name. The fragment is the first to refer to Pythagoras' political convictions and says that he left Samos at the age of forty and migrated to Italy because he abhorred the tyranny established by Polykrates; he thought it unbecoming a lover of liberty to submit to such a rule.

The fragment is also interesting because it contains a chronological statement. There is, of course, no possibility of finding out from what kind of evidence Aristoxenos derived his knowledge of Pythagoras' age. There is the instance of Xenophanes, who in his poems mentioned his age in connection with certain historical events; and the way in which he does it seems to indicate that this was not entirely uncommon in the sixth century. But the case of Pythagoras, who did not

[24] Cf. p. 10.
[25] Diog. Laert. I, 11, 118.

publish any works, is different, and though the "canon" of Apollodoros, by which the ἀκμή is identified with the age of forty and usually synchronized with an important event in the life of an author, scarcely goes back to the time of Aristoxenos, it is quite possible that Aristoxenos did not imply much more than a *floruit* and that the date given by him was derived from rather general considerations. Yet it is worth while to notice that obviously, in his opinion, Pythagoras was no longer a young man in the decade between 540 and 530.

The whole fragment recurs in only slightly different wording in a long extract from the novel of Antonius Diogenes in Porphyrios 16. This confirms the view that other parts of this extract, as for instance the second fragment,[26] are also ultimately derived from Aristoxenos. But Diogenes has mixed the different traditions, legends, and fables to such an extent that no further inferences as to the part which derives from Aristoxenos can be drawn from this observation.

(4) In Section 22 Porphyrios quotes Aristoxenos as saying that Lucanians, Messapians, Peuketians, and even Romans were attracted by the fame of Pythagoras and came to seek his advice. This quotation occurs in a passage which as a whole is taken from Nikomachos, who made great use of the work of Aristoxenos.[27] The quotation is preceded by a passage which states that Pythagoras found the cities of Southern Italy and Sicily δεδουλωμένας ὑπ' ἀλλήλων, τὰς μὲν πολλῶν ἐτῶν, τὰς δὲ νεωστί, that he filled them—Kroton, Sybaris, Katane, Rhegion, Himera, Akragas, and Tauromenion are mentioned —with a spirit of freedom and gave them laws through Charondas and Zaleukos, and that Simichos, the tyrant of Kentoripe, laid down his rule voluntarily under Pythagorean influence and distributed his wealth, giving it to his sister and his fellow citizens.

[26] Cf. p. 17.
[27] Cf. Appendix B.

ARISTOXENOS AND DIKAIARCHOS 19

The quotation from Aristoxenos is followed by a passage stating that Pythagoras succeeded in removing all στάσις not only from the Pythagoreans of his time but also from their ἀπόγονοι for many generations and, in addition, from the Southern Italian and Sicilian cities both in their internal affairs and in their mutual relations. The question, therefore, arises whether this whole passage derives from Aristoxenos or only the words in which he is quoted.

This question is not easy to decide. The whole chapter recurs almost literally in Iamblichos 34, but here the passage about the removal of all στάσις follows immediately the sentence about Pythagoras' influence on the constitutions of Italian and Sicilian towns, while the notice on the Lucanians, Messapians, etc., for which Aristoxenos is expressly quoted in Porphyrios, is inserted much later under the heading: Ἐπεὶ δὲ κατὰ γένη τεταγμένως οὕτω διήλθομεν περὶ Πυθαγόρου καὶ τῶν Πυθαγορείων, ἴθι δὴ τὸ μετὰ τοῦτο καὶ τὰς σποράδην ἀφηγήσεις εἰωθυίας λέγεσθαι ποιησώμεθα, ὅσαι οὐχ ὑποπίπτουσιν ὑπὸ τὴν προειρημένην τάξιν.[28] This seems to suggest that Porphyrios or the anonymous biography which he used inserted the quotation from Aristoxenos in a context which was taken from some other author. For the two other sentences of the chapter obviously belonged from the outset to the same account. On the other hand, these two sentences can scarcely have followed each other in the original since they refer to two very different epochs in Pythagoras' life and the notice on the Lucanians fits very aptly into the extract. Also the omission of a sentence of the work which he is using and its insertion in some other place is by no means unique in the work of Iamblichos.[29]

[28] Iambl. 241.
[29] One may also point out that a quotation from Aristoxenos, one of the most important authors on the life of Pythagoras, can scarcely be considered as one of the σποράδην ἀφηγήσεις. Yet Iamblichos quotes

Since the problem cannot be solved in this way it becomes necessary to look for other criteria. One criterion may be found in an observation made by Mewaldt.[30] He has pointed out that the laws of Zaleukos and Charondas are mentioned in connection with Pythagoras' activity in Southern Italy in a quotation from Aristoxenos' Νόμοι παιδευτικοί in Diogenes Laertios VII, 1, 16. This makes it very likely that the first part of the Nikomachos chapter in Porphyrios 22 is also derived from Aristoxenos. The other criterion may be found in the observation that here again we have the same tendency as in the other quotations from Aristoxenos: to represent Pythagoras as a bringer of freedom and peace.

One might object that the last sentence of the chapter, which cannot be separated from its first part, is at variance with the story about the Kylonian troubles in the long fragment, Sections 248–51. But one must take into consideration that Aristoxenos is of all the ancient authors the only one who represents the troubles that started in the lifetime of Pythagoras as of relatively little importance and who says expressly[31] that, in spite of them, law and order continued to prevail for a long period, and that even when the rebellion broke out it remained confined to the city of Kroton.

This shows that, notwithstanding the seeming contradiction between Iamblichos 34 and Sections 248 ff., these two accounts are still very closely related. If the first of them can be understood *cum grano salis* they may still have the same origin, since there are so many indications that point in this direction. In the first of these accounts, however, the original has obviously been so much shortened that it is no longer

---

under this heading the one sentence which Porphyrios assigns to Aristoxenos by name. This shows that Iamblichos' excerpts must have been disarranged.

[30] *Op. cit.*, pp. 34 ff.
[31] Iambl. 249.

possible to determine with certainty how much the expression μέχρι πολλῶν γενεῶν was originally meant to imply. This is very unfortunate; for otherwise it would be very helpful as an indication as to whether Aristoxenos dated the catastrophe at Kroton in the middle or in the later part of the fifth century.

Even so the fragment is interesting because here again we find the view that the influence of Pythagoras and the Pythagoreans extended over a large area and a great number of cities, but that it did not imply the domination, or even the hegemony, of one city over others, or a government by compulsion in any single city, but that, on the contrary, the Pythagoreans worked for the establishment of a liberal regime everywhere.

(5) Diogenes Laertios[32] enumerates the last Pythagoreans who preserved the old customs and doctrines at the time when the order was gradually dying out, and says that Aristoxenos knew them personally. There can be scarcely any doubt that this fact was mentioned by Aristoxenos himself.

(6) There is only one more fragment for which Aristoxenos is quoted by name. It has come down to Iamblichos[33] and Porphyrios[34] through Nikomachos and contains the famous story of Dionysios the younger and the two Pythagorean friends Damon and Phintias. Nikomachos says that Aristoxenos claims to have heard the story from Dionysios himself, who used to tell it at the time when, having been deprived of his rule at Syracuse, he lived as a teacher at Korinth.

The wording of the story in Iamblichos and Porphyrios differs only slightly, but Iamblichos says that Aristoxenos told it in his work Περὶ τοῦ Πυθαγορικοῦ βίου, while Porphyrios states that it is taken from his Βίος Πυθαγόρου. Obviously

[32] VIII, 1, 46.
[33] 234-237.
[34] 59-60.

neither of them was aware of the fact that these are two different works by the same author.[35] This proves not only that neither author knew even so much as the titles of Aristoxenos' works except through the quotations in other authors, but also that they both indulged in the habit of many ancient authors of adopting and, so to speak, taking possession of excerpts made from the works of others by slightly altering the wording, not noticing in many cases that they were actually changing the meaning also. As to the special case in question, Mewaldt[36] contends with probability that Iamblichos is right and that the story was taken from the work Περὶ τοῦ Πυθαγορικοῦ βίου.

(7) There are two other fragments referring to the same epoch which can be attributed to Aristoxenos with certainty, though his name is not mentioned in connection with them. These are the two stories about Archytas and Kleinias in Iamblichos 197 and 198, which, according to the author, Aristoxenos' father Spintharos used to tell. Since these anecdotes are of no historical importance whatever, but illustrate Pythagorean maxims and customs, they too are obviously taken from the work Περὶ τοῦ Πυθαγορικοῦ βίου.

It would not have been worth while to mention these last two fragments if they had not some bearing on the question of what traces of the work of Aristoxenos can be found in the tenth book of Diodoros. E. Schwartz in his famous article on Diodoros[37] has pointed out that Diodoros must have made

[35] Mewaldt (*op. cit.*, p. 3) has shown that there existed four different works of Aristoxenos, all dealing with Pythagoreanism: 1. The Βίος Πυθαγόρου καὶ τῶν γνωρίμων αὐτοῦ, usually cited as Βίος Πυθαγόρου; this work contained a biography of Pythagoras and a history of the Pythagoreans in chronological order. 2. The Περὶ Πυθαγορικοῦ βίου; this work dealt with the practical application of Pythagorean principles and contained many anecdotes illustrating Pythagorean friendship, chastity, frugality, etc. 3. The Πυθαγορικαὶ ἀποφάσεις. 4. The Νόμοι παιδευτικοί.
[36] *Op. cit.*, pp. 25–26.
[37] Pauly-Wissowa, V, 679.

considerable use of Aristoxenos' works in his account of the history of the Pythagoreans, since there are many striking similarities with fragments attributed to Aristoxenos by Iamblichos and Porphyrios. He has however also drawn attention to the fact that Diodoros cannot have taken his information from Aristoxenos directly, since in one place a quotation from Kallimachos is interwoven in the narrative.

The question requires some further investigation. The resemblance is most striking between Diodoros X, 7, iv and the Spintharos story in Iamblichos 197. The other story which is attributed to Spintharos by Iamblichos[38] does not recur in Diodoros. But Diodoros tells a different story of the same Kleinias who is the hero of this excerpt from the work of Aristoxenos. That this is no mere coincidence can be proved by the following observations. The story told about Kleinias in Diodoros X, 4 recurs in Iamblichos 230 together with other stories about Pythagorean friendship. In Iamblichos 129 we find the words[39]: καὶ τὰ περὶ Φιντίαν καὶ Δάμωνα περί τε Πλάτωνα καὶ Ἀρχύταν καὶ τὰ περὶ Κλεινίαν καὶ Πρῶρον. This is an enumeration of stories about Pythagorean friendship, of which the first is expressly quoted as Aristoxenian by Iamblichos and Porphyrios, while the second is very likely to have formed part of his work, considering his close personal relation to both Plato and Archytas. If one further takes into account that Kleinias is not mentioned by any other ancient author but was a personal friend of Spintharos who liked to tell anecdotes about him, there can be scarcely any doubt that the Kleinias-Proros story, the story told by Diodoros, has also the same origin.

A further coincidence between Diodoros and Aristoxenos can be found in the Damon-Phintias story[40] itself, but in this

---
[38] 198.
[39] The first part of the sentence is corrupt, and there is probably a lacuna in the context.
[40] Diod. X, 4, iii.

case a closer examination shows that Diodoros has not preserved the story in its original form. The story as told by Aristoxenos is rather involved and complicated. Phintias has not really conspired against Dionysios nor did he really want to kill him. The plot is made by Dionysios and his friends who accuse him falsely of conspiring against the life of the tyrant, because they want to find out whether the current stories about Pythagorean friendship are true. The rest of the story is the same as in all the other versions. When Phintias is condemned to death he asks for permission to absent himself for a few days, and his friend Damon pledges his own life for him. In the end he proves by returning in the last moment that Pythagorean friendship is equal to any test.

If the story is told in this way one asks with some surprise how Dionysios could know that Phintias would ask for a leave and beg his friend to pledge his own life for him. For if he did not know this he could not expect a test of friendship to arise out of Phintias' arrest, which, according to this version, was his purpose in accusing him. Whether there was any indication in the work of Aristoxenos as to how this question is to be answered we do not know. In any case the story is more complicated when told in this way.

On the other hand, the tendency is obvious. The Pythagorean is not to be represented as a conspirator or a potential murderer, even of a tyrant. Again the tendency is apologetic, but there is a new element in it. In the other fragments of Aristoxenos the Pythagoreans are represented as lovers of liberty and as opposed to tyrannical regimes. Since ancient democrats in general considered the assassination of tyrants as a laudable deed, one might think that the Aristoxenian version of the Phintias story is at variance with the tendency of his other fragments. But this is not the case. In Aristoxenos' account Pythagoras does not try to overthrow the tyranny of Polykrates by force; much less does he make an attempt to kill him; instead he leaves Samos, because it is not becoming

ARISTOXENOS AND DIKAIARCHOS

to a free man to live under such a regime. In Italy too he does not persuade the people to abolish tyrannical regimes by force, but he succeeds in persuading a tyrant to give up his rule voluntarily and establishes liberal governments elsewhere by equally peaceful means.[41] Even after the terrible disaster at Kroton the Pythagoreans make no attempt to take revenge, though they seem to hope that the "cities" may come to their aid. There can be no doubt that in all this there is the same very marked and conscious tendency. The Pythagoreans are represented as favoring liberal government, but at the same time they are depicted as so much opposed to violence that they prefer to leave their country in order to avoid the alternative of submitting to tyranny or opposing it by force. This makes it almost certain that all the fragments in which this tendency can be noticed, are derived from the same source.[42]

The Damon-Phintias story as told by Diodoros is different. There is no conspiracy of Dionysios and his friends, but Phintias has really the intention to assassinate the tyrant. The story becomes much simpler, but the tendency characteristic of all the Aristoxenian fragments has disappeared. This must make us very cautious in attributing to Aristoxenos without restriction the accounts of Pythagorean history given by Diodoros.

Another instance of the same kind is provided by Diodoros X, 3: Επ' ἄρχοντος 'Αθήνησιν Θηρικλέους κατὰ τὴν ἑξηκοστὴν πρώτην 'Ολυμπιάδα Πυθαγόρας ὁ φιλόσοφος ἐγνωρίζετο προκεκοφὼς ἤδη ἐν παιδείᾳ. This passage has obviously some connection with the Aristoxenos passage in Porphyrios 9, which states that Pythagoras left Samos at the age of forty. For with Diodoros, as with most other ancient authors following the "canon" of Apollodoros, ἐγνωρίζετο usually refers to a man's

---
[41] Cf. Chapter V, footnote 4.
[42] In the course of this inquiry it will become clear how much all the other ancient authors differ from Aristoxenos in this respect.

ἀκμή, that is the time when he was about forty; the words προκεκοφὼς ἤδη ἐν παιδείᾳ are then in perfect harmony with the account given by Aristoxenos, and the early years of the reign of Polykrates to which Aristoxenos refers include the date given by Diodoros. On the other hand, for general reasons as well as from the passage in Porphyrios it is obvious that Aristoxenos did not mention the Olympiad nor the Attic archon, though the latter method of determining dates, but not the first, was occasionally used by Aristotle and Theophrastos. One has therefore to assume that a συγχρονισμός given by Aristoxenos has been used in order to arrive at a more definite date by means of calculation.[43]

It is in the light of these facts that Diodoros' account of Pythagoras' sojourn in Delos has to be considered. For Diodoros' version of this story seems to be a compromise between Aristoxenos, who (as shown above) dated the event in the time when Pythagoras still lived in Samos, and those authors who dated it in the time of the disaster at Kroton. He assumes that Pherekydes died when Pythagoras had already migrated to Italy, but during the earlier part of his sojourn there, and obviously long before the Krotonian catastrophe occurred, since he relates this event much later.

All this shows that most of Diodoros' material in the tenth book concerning the Pythagoreans is ultimately derived from Aristoxenos, but has frequently not been preserved in its original form, as it appears, for example, in Iamblichos and Porphyrios; on the contrary, it has undergone a number of alterations. In some cases it is very likely that there were several successive alterations, made by different authors, until the story took the shape in which it is told by Diodoros.

[43] The origin of this passage in the work of Diodoros is probably very complicated. A. Rostagni (*Atti della R. Accademia delle scienze di Torino*, XLIX [1914], 378) has tried to prove that it is partly influenced by Timaios. But Timaios did not date in this year the ἀκμή of Pythagoras but only his migration to Italy. Diodoros' chronology seems, therefore, to be a combination of Aristoxenos and Timaios.

CHAPTER II

The Sources of Dikaiarchos and Aristoxenos and
The Reliability of Their Accounts

HAVING made a survey of the fragments that can be attributed to Aristoxenos with certainty and of his influence on certain later authors, we may turn to the question of the identification of the primary sources from which Aristoxenos derived his knowledge. Delatte has drawn attention to the significance of the fact that, according to Diogenes Laertios VIII, 46, Aristoxenos knew personally the "last Pythagoreans" whom he mentions at the end of the long historical account in Iamblichos 248 ff. This, together with the marked apologetic tendency that can be noticed everywhere in his fragments, makes it very likely indeed that he got much if not nearly all of his information from them. This conclusion of Delatte will be confirmed later on by further evidence.

In order to find this evidence we have to ask first what these last Pythagoreans are likely to have known best, and therefore who they were and when they lived.

Fortunately there is among the men mentioned by Diogenes Laertios at least one, Echekrates, who can be dated within certain limits. Plato makes him one of the interlocutors in the introductory dialogue of the *Phaedo*. The passage[1] leaves

[1] *Phaedo* 57a.

no doubt that, when Echekrates and Phaidon meet at Phleius, a comparatively short time has passed since the death of Sokrates. For nobody has come to Phleius from Athens in the meantime nor has any Phliasian visited Athens to tell the whole story of Sokrates' death. Echekrates therefore can scarcely have been younger than Phaidon, who in the year 399 was about 18 years old. On the other hand, since Aristoxenos, who was younger than Aristotle (born 487), knew Echekrates personally, he cannot have been older than Archytas, the older contemporary of Plato. Consequently he belonged to about the same generation as Archytas, though he may have been a decade younger, but not much more. He was a friend of one of the youngest followers of Sokrates and probably of about the same age as Spintharos, who is also said to have known Sokrates personally. All these different traditions are in perfect harmony.

Thus one can draw the final conclusion that the so-called last Pythagoreans, since they belong to the same generation as Archytas and since we find them living in continental Greece at the beginning of the fourth century, are either identical with the group which, according to Iamblichos 251, emigrated from Italy when Archytas was the only one to stay, or must at least have been in close contact with this group. This agrees also with the chronology given by Diodoros,[2] who dates the last Pythagoreans in 367 (Ol. 103, 3), that is, the time when Archytas took a leading part in shaping a common policy of the Greek cities of Southern Italy. These Pythagoreans therefore must have been perfectly familiar with the events that happened during the last years of the fifth and the first half of the fourth century.

Since Lysis, who was the adviser of young Epaminondas, cannot have died earlier than 390 (probably he did not die before 385) and since the tradition is full of stories about the

[2] XV, 76, iv.

way in which the Pythagoreans of the fourth century tried to resume relations with Lysis in his old age, one should also assume that they took some pains to obtain firsthand information concerning the events at Kroton at which he had been present and which marked the most decisive stage in the history of the Pythagorean order. Under these circumstances it is very significant that Aristoxenos is able to distinguish three different periods in the political history of the Pythagoreans after the time of the disaster at Kroton—the time about which the last Pythagoreans are likely to have had special information—while the account which he gives of the period between Pythagoras' death and the destruction of the house of Milon is extremely vague.

Let us then try to draw some conclusions concerning the reliability of the different parts of Aristoxenos' account. It is obvious that those parts of his story which deal with the time of the last Pythagoreans or with the time of Lysis, with whom they were in contact, are likely to be not only more detailed, but also more reliable on the whole, than his account of earlier times. But this obvious distinction is not sufficient. In the second part of his story, one must further distinguish between (1) those facts told by him which are morally and politically indifferent, (2) those facts which are apt to throw some light on the moral and political principles of the Pythagoreans, and (3) the moral and political interpretation of these facts.

As to the first group it is obvious that an account based on personal recollections of the last Pythagoreans, or on information obtained by them from their personal teachers or elder associates will be preferable to any other tradition unless this be derived from unquestionable documents of the time to which it refers. This applies especially to the chronological order of events[3] and the account of different periods in the

[3] Notice that the chronology is established by means of synchronisms

history of the later Pythagoreans. There can be no doubt, for instance, that Aristoxenos' dating of the Krotonian catastrophe deserves more credence than the popular tradition, represented by Dikaiarchos among others,[4] which dates this event in the lifetime of Pythagoras. Aristoxenos obviously knows that it must be later, since Lysis took part in it, but he knows as little about the time that elapsed between the death of Pythagoras and the disaster at Kroton as the popular tradition does and therefore fills in the gap with difficulty by vague expressions like μέχρι τινός, τέλος δὲ, etc.

As to the second group one has to be much more skeptical. According to Aristoxenos there has been no revolution against the Pythagoreans, except in Kroton. The other cities merely refused to support them against their Krotonian enemies. The popular tradition, on the contrary, knows of upheavals and rebellions against the Pythagoreans all over Southern Italy. Now it is a well-known fact that popular tradition everywhere tends to increase the importance and extent of events that made a great impression at their time and changed the course of history. But it is doubtful whether one single event that was confined to one single city, terrifying and important as it may have been, would have been sufficient to create legends of similar events which were supposed to have happened in all the important cities in Southern Italy and to give rise to so general an expression as the πανταχοῦ γὰρ ἐγένοντο μεγάλαι στάσεις, ἃς ἔτι καὶ νῦν . . . . μνημονεύονται κτλ. of Dikaiarchos. The Pythagoreans, on the other hand, had every reason to make the rebellion appear as restricted as possible. For while in one single city or political unit long-nourished

---

and that we are much less liable to error in remembering synchronisms than in remembering dates.

[4] Cf. the words ἃς ἔτι καὶ νῦν οἱ περὶ τοὺς τόπους μνημονεύονται καὶ διηγοῦνται in the Dikaiarchos fragment in Porph. 56. His story of how Pythagoras was saved is obviously legendary.

party hatred or even the resentment of one single influential individual may lead to anything, it would be difficult to believe that the personal ambition and resentment of one single man, Kylon, could have caused a persecution in a great many independent cities all over Southern Italy, and this many years after his death.

As to the interpretation of events, we are of course at perfect liberty to reinterpret them entirely if the factual evidence provided by Aristoxenos and other ancient sources should make this necessary.[5]

To sum up, then, one may say that in all chronological questions as well as in the question whether a certain historical personality was directly or indirectly involved in a certain event Aristoxenos must be considered as the most reliable authority—at least as far as the period after about 450 is concerned—since the men from whom he got his information must have been extremely well acquainted with these facts and had no special reason to distort them. The popular tradition, on the other hand, which is represented by Dikaiarchos, is apt to be very confused in matters of this kind.

Concerning the political character of the party strife which led to the revolution against the Pythagoreans and the geographical extent of this revolution Aristoxenos' account is not very likely to be quite reliable, since his authorities were obviously biased in this respect. Concerning these questions,

[5] That the interpretation of earlier events given by the last Pythagoreans was in some cases greatly biased is well illustrated by Aristoxenos' statement (cf. p. 18) that Pythagoras liberated Sybaris from tyrannical rule. One of the best-established facts in the Southern Italian history of those times is the destruction of Sybaris. Up to the time of the catastrophe Sybaris had been under the rule of the tyrant or king (cf. Freeman, *History of Sicily*, II, Appendix I) Telys (cf. Herodotos V, 44; Diod. XII, 9; Athenaios XII, 21, p. 521 f.). The downfall of Sybaris therefore coincided with the downfall of Telys' rule. To call the destruction of a city her liberation from tyranny reveals certainly some political bias.

on the other hand, Dikaiarchos may very well be used as a supplementary source. For the memory of the fact *that* a certain event happened in a place is very likely to stay alive in that special place at a time when the date of the event and the persons who took part in it have been long forgotten.

If this is taken into consideration Aristoxenos and Dikaiarchos, both of whom show no trace of literary embellishments, inventions, or falsifications, in spite of their discrepancies, may be used together in the attempt to reconstruct the political history of the Pythagoreans.

But there is one more author whose fragments have to be collected and analyzed since his work is of extreme importance for this reconstruction: Timaios of Tauromenium. As to the wealth of later "tradition" A. Delatte[6] has shown conclusively that almost all the allusions found in later authors like Athenagoras, Origen, Hippolytos, Arnobius, Firmicus Maternus, Themistios, the Suidas Lexicon, etc., can be traced back either to Diogenes Laertios, Iamblichos, and Porphyrios directly, or to their sources; hence it is not necessary to take up this part of the investigation again.

[6] *Op. cit.*, pp. 230 ff.

CHAPTER III

Reconstruction of Timaios' Version and the Reliability of His Accounts

ALMOST the whole tradition on the early Pythagoreans found in Polybios, Justinus, and Diodoros XI and XII and a very large part of those sections of the works of Iamblichos and Porphyrios which are derived from neither Aristoxenos nor Dikaiarchos have been attributed to Timaios by one or the other modern scholar.[1] The evidence on which these attributions rest, however, is of an entirely different type from the evidence which had been available in the case of Aristoxenos. For, apart from the few cases in which Aristoxenos' father is cited as the authority, Aristoxenos is always quoted by name, and these quotations themselves are obviously all of them more or less literal if frequently shortened. The only question that could arise in most of the cases was therefore how far a fragment extends and whether the fact

[1] Important studies in the questions discussed in this chapter are: E. Rohde, *Kleine Schriften*, II, 133 ff.; A. Kothe, *De Timaei Tauromenitani vita et scriptis* (Dissert., Breslau, 1874); A. Delatte, *Revue de l'instruction publique en Belgique*, LII (1909), 90 ff.—to be referred to henceforth as Delatte (*R*); A. Delatte, *Musée belge*, XVIII (1920), 5 ff.—to be referred to henceforth as Delatte (*M*); A. Delatte, *Bibliothèque de la Faculté de Liége*, XXIX, 213 ff.—to be referred to henceforth as Delatte (*B*); A. Rostagni, *Atti della R. Accademia delle scienze di Torino*, XLIX (1914), 373 ff. and 554 ff.

that the original is shortened has caused a distortion of the original connection of the historical facts. And even in answering these questions one is greatly helped by the marked political tendency of all genuine Aristoxenian fragments, since this makes it comparatively easy to decide what comes from this source and what does not.

All this is very different in the case of Timaios. There are only a very few fragments concerning the Pythagoreans for which Timaios is quoted by name. None of these fragments contains any facts pertaining to the political history of the Pythagoreans. But extensive use has been made of them by modern scholars in an attempt to identify other passages in ancient authors as Timean. Among these latter there are passages of very great historical interest.

Yet there is no likelihood in any of the cases in which a later ancient author has used the work of Timaios without quoting him that the original wording is preserved. The most extensive extracts from the work of Timaios have come down to us through Polybios, Justinus (i.e., Pompeius Trogus), and Diodoros. Polybios and Trogus never quote their sources literally but always remold the tradition so as to adapt it to the style and purpose of their own works. The same, though to a lesser degree, is also true of Diodoros.[2] The rest of the Timean fragments are known to us through Iamblichos and Porphyrios. But while these authors drew their knowledge of the versions of Aristoxenos and Dikaiarchos from Neanthes and Nikomachos who usually quote their sources literally, they obtained the fragments of the Timean version which we find in their works through Apollonios of Tyana and Antonius Diogenes, who follow, with much less truly historical spirit, the method of Polybios and Trogus.

All this shows quite clearly that in the case of Timaios the task is much more difficult, and a different method of investi-

[2] Cf. pp. 23-27.

gation will have to be followed. Nor is it surprising that the scholars who tried to reconstruct the share of Timaios in the later tradition arrived at widely differing results.

Yet the situation is not quite so hopeless as it may appear at first sight, and in any case the problem cannot be neglected. For the different parts of later tradition have to be weighed; and it makes a very great difference whether or not they can be traced to Timaios, who lived at a comparatively early time, who made investigations on the spot, who was known for his interest in genuine old documents, and to whom much genuine information may have still been available which could not have been acquired by a later author. In addition, it is obvious that the accounts given by Polybios, Diodoros, Justinus, and Apollonios of Tyana (in Iamblichos and Porphyrios) have many interconnections which cannot be explained except through the assumption of common sources. Some investigation into the character of these sources must therefore be made whether the author can be identified in every case or not. Here, as in the case of Aristoxenos, it will be the special aim of the present inquiry to distinguish carefully between those results which are incontestable and those which have only a higher or lower degree of probability.

To begin with, it will be necessary to place side by side the fragments of Timaios which deal with Pythagoras and the Pythagoreans and the passages of later authors which coincide with them in contents and partly in wording without mentioning Timaios' name (see Parallels II, III, IV, V).

A glance at these parallels shows that Timaios has been used many times by later authors either directly or indirectly without being quoted. But even where he is quoted by name for the same statement by different authors, much less of the original wording, if any, is preserved[3] than in the case of the

[3] The closest resemblance exists between Schol. Plat. *Phaedr.* 279c and Iambl. 72 (see Parallel V).

PARALLEL II

Iamblichos 17σ	Timaios, Fr. 78 M = Porphyrios, Vita Pythagorae 4	Favorinus in Diogenes Laertios VIII, 15	Justinus XX, 4, xvii–xviii
Φασὶ τοίνυν αὐτὸν τὸν Πυθαγόραν κληρονομήσαντα τὸν Ἀλκαίου βίον τοῦ μετὰ τὴν εἰς Λακεδαίμονα πρεσβείαν τὸν βίον καταλύσαντος, οὐδὲν ἧττον θαυμασθῆναι κατὰ τὴν οἰκονομίαν ἢ τὴν φιλοσοφίαν, γήμαντα δὲ τὴν γεννηθεῖσαν αὐτῷ θυγατέρα, μετὰ ταῦτα Μένωνι τῷ Κροτωνιάτῃ συνοικήσασαν, ἀγαγεῖν οὕτως, ὥστε παρθένον οὖσαν ἡγεῖσθαι τῶν χορῶν, γυναῖκα δὲ γενομένην πρώτην προσιέναι τοῖς βωμοῖς, τοὺς δὲ Μεταποντίνους διὰ μνήμην ἔτι ἔχοντας τὸν Πυθαγόραν μετὰ τοὺς αὐτοῦ χρόνους τὴν μὲν οἰκίαν αὐτοῦ Δήμητρος ἱερὸν καλέσαι, τὸν δὲ στενωπὸν Μουσεῖον.	Τίμαιος δ᾽ἱστορεῖ τὴν Πυθαγόρου θυγατέρα καὶ παρθένον οὖσαν ἡγεῖσθαι τῶν παρθένων ἐν Κρότωνι καὶ γυναῖκα γυναικῶν, τὴν δὲ οἰκίαν Δήμητρος ἱερὸν ποιῆσαι τοὺς Κροτωνιάτας, τὸν δὲ στενωπὸν καλεῖν Μουσεῖον.	Μεταποντῖνοι μὲν οὖν τὴν μὲν οἰκίαν αὐτοῦ Δήμητρος ἱερὸν ἐκάλουν, τὸν δὲ στενωπὸν Μουσεῖον, ὥς φησι Φαβωρῖνος ἐν παντοδαπῇ ἱστορίᾳ.	Pythagoras autem, cum annos XX Crotonae egisset, Metapontum migravit ibique decessit; cuius tanta admiratio fuit, ut ex domo eius templum facerent eumque pro deo colerent.

Parallel III

Iamblichos 56	Timaios, Fr. 83 M = Diogenes Laertios VIII, 11	Justinus XX, 4, xviii ff.
Ἔτι δὲ τὸν σοφώτατον τῶν ἁπάντων λεγόμενον καὶ συντάξαντα τὴν φωνὴν τῶν ἀνθρώπων καὶ τὸ σύνολον εὑρετὴν καταστάντα τῶν ὀνομάτων, εἴτε θεὸν εἴτε δαίμονα, εἴτε θεῖόν τινα ἄνθρωπον, συνιδόντα ὅτι τῆς εὐσεβείας οἰκειότατόν ἐστι τὸ γένος τῶν γυναικῶν, ἑκάστην τὴν ἡλικίαν αὐτῶν συνώνυμον ποιήσασθαι θεῷ καὶ καλέσαι τὴν μὲν ἄγαμον Κόρην, τὴν δὲ πρὸς ἄνδρα δεδομένην Νύμφην, τὴν δὲ τέκνα γεννησαμένην Μητέρα, τὴν δὲ παῖδα ἐκ παιδῶν ἐπιδοῦσαν .... Μαῖαν. ᾧ σύμφωνον εἶναι καὶ τοὺς χρησμοὺς ἐν Δωδώνῃ καὶ Δελφοῖς δηλοῦσθαι διὰ γυναικός. Διὰ δὲ τῶν εἰς τὴν εὐσέβειαν ἐπαίνων πρὸς τὴν εὐτέλειαν τὴν κατὰ τὸν ἱματισμὸν τηλικαύτην παρασκευάσαι τὴν μεταβολὴν ὥστε τὰ πολυτελῆ τῶν ἱματίων μηδεμίαν ἐνδύεσθαι, ἀλλὰ θεῖναι πάσας εἰς τὸ τῆς Ἥρας ἱερὸν πολλὰς μυριάδας ἱματίων.	Τίμαιός τέ φησιν ἐν δεκάτῃ ἱστοριῶν λέγειν αὐτὸν [sc. Πυθαγόραν.] τὰς συνοικούσας ἀνδράσι θεῶν ἔχειν ὀνόματα, Κόρας, Νύμφας, εἶτα Μητέρας καλουμένας	Inter haec velut genetricem virtutum *frugalitatem* omnibus ingerebat consecutusque disputationum adsiduitate erat, ut matronae *auratas vestes* ceteraque dignitatis suae ornamenta velut luxuriae instrumenta *deponerent* eaque *omnia delata in Iunonis aedem ipsi deae consecrarent*, prae se ferentes vera ornamenta matronarum pudicitiam, non vestes, esse.

Parallel IV

Iamblichos 35	Macrobius, Sat. III, 6	Timaios, Fr. 79 = Censorinus, De die nat. 2	Iamblichos 25 (Apollonios)	Justinus XX, 4
Εἰ δὲ δεῖ καὶ τὰ καθ' ἕκαστον ἀπομνημονεῦσαι ὧν [Πυθαγόρας] ἔπραξε καὶ εἶπε ῥητέον ὡς παρεγένετο μὲν εἰς Ἰταλίαν κατὰ τὴν Ὀλυμπιάδα τὴν δευτέραν ἐπὶ ταῖς ἑξήκοντα καθ' ἣν Ἐρυξίας ὁ Χαλκιδεὺς στάδιον ἐνίκησεν, εὐθὺς δὲ περιβλέπτος καὶ περίστατος ἐγένετο, καθάπερ καὶ πρότερον ὅτε εἰς Δῆλον κατέπλευσεν. Ἐκεῖ γὰρ πρὸς μόνον τὸν βωμὸν τὸν τοῦ γενέτορος Ἀπόλλωνος προσευξάμενος ὃς μόνος ἀναίμακτός ἐστιν ἐθαυμάσθη παρὰ τοῖς ἐν τῇ νήσῳ	Deli ara est Apollinis Γενέτορος in qua nullum animal sacrificatur, quam Pythagoram velut inviolatam adoravisse produnt.	Denique Deli ad Apollinis genitoris aram, ut Timaeus auctor est, nemo hostiam caedit.	Λέγεται δὲ περὶ τὸν αὐτὸν χρόνον [his second stay at Samos] θαυμασθῆναι αὐτὸν περὶ τὴν Δῆλον, προσελθόντα πρὸς τὸν ἀναίμακτον λεγόμενον καὶ τοῦ Γενέτορος Ἀπόλλωνος βωμὸν καὶ τοῦτον θεραπεύσαντα. Ὅθεν εἰς πάντα τὰ μαντεῖα παρέβαλε. Καὶ ἐν Κρήτῃ καὶ ἐν Σπάρτῃ τῶν νόμων ἕνεκα διέτριψε.	Inde regressus [sc. from Egypt] Cretam et Lacedaemona ad cognoscendas Minois et Lycurgi inclytas ea tempestate leges contenderat.

PARALLEL V

Iamblichos 71	Scholia in Platonis Phaedrum 279 (Vol. VI, 275 Hermann)	Timaios, Fr. 77 = Diogenes Laertios VIII, 10	Iamblichos 72
Παρεσκευασμένῳ δὲ αὐτῷ οὕτως εἰς τὴν παιδείαν τῶν ὁμιλητῶν προσιόντων τῶν ἑτέρων καὶ βουλομένων συνδιατρίβειν οὐκ εὐθὺς συνεχώρει, μέχρις ἂν αὐτῶν τὴν δοκιμασίαν καὶ τὴν κρίσιν ποιήσεται.	Φησὶ γοῦν ὁ Τίμαιος ἐν τῇ Ε οὕτω· προσιόντων δ᾽ οὖν αὐτῷ τῶν νεωτέρων καὶ βουλομένων συνδιατρίβειν οὐκ εὐθὺς συνεχώρησεν, ἀλλ᾽ ἔφη δεῖν καὶ τὰς οὐσίας κοινὰς εἶναι τῶν ἐντυγχανόντων. Εἶτα μεταπολλὰ φησὶ καὶ δι᾽ ἐκείνους πρῶτον ῥηθῆναι κατὰ τὴν Ἰταλίαν ὅτι κοινὰ τὰ τῶν φίλων.	Εἶπε δὲ πρῶτος [sc. Πυθαγόρας], ὥς φησι Τίμαιος, κοινὰ τὰ φίλων εἶναι καὶ φιλίαν ἰσότητα. Καὶ αὐτοῦ οἱ μαθηταὶ κατετίθεντο τὰς οὐσίας εἰς ἕν. πενταετίαν δ᾽ ἡσύχαζον, μόνον τῶν λόγων ἀκούοντες καὶ οὐδέπω Πυθαγόραν ὁρῶντες εἰς ὃ δοκιμασθεῖεν.	Καὶ ὅντινα δοκιμάσειεν οὕτως, ἐφίει τριῶν ἐτῶν ὑπεροράσθαι δοκιμάζων πῶς ἔχει βεβαιότητος . . . . Μετὰ δὲ τοῦτο τοῖς προσιοῦσι προσέταττε σιωπὴν πενταετῆ ἀποπειρώμενος πῶς ἐγκρατῶς ἔχουσιν.
Iamblichos 81			
Τῶν μὲν οὖν Πυθαγορείων κοινὴν εἶναι τὴν οὐσίαν διέταξε καὶ τὴν συμβίωσιν ἅμα διὰ παντὸς τοῦ χρόνου διατελεῖν, τοὺς δὲ ἑτέρους ἰδίας μὲν κτήσεις ἔχειν ἐκέλευσε, συνιόντας δὲ εἰς ταὐτὸ συσχολάζειν ἀλλήλοις.	Cf. Phot. Lex. 129: Κοινὰ τὰ φίλων. Τιμαιός φησι ἐν τῇ Θ ταύτην λεχθῆναι κατὰ τὴν Μεγάλην Ἑλλάδα καθ᾽ οὓς χρόνους Πυθαγόρας ἀνέπειθεν τοὺς ταύτην ἐνοικοῦντας ἀδιανέμητα κεκτῆσθαι.		Ἐν τούτῳ δὴ τῷ χρόνῳ τὰ μὲν ἑκάστου ὑπάρχοντα, τουτέστιν αἱ οὐσίαι, ἐκοινοῦντο. . . . . Μετὰ τὴν πενταετῆ σιωπὴν ἐσωτερικοὶ ἐγίγνοντο καὶ ἐντὸς συνδόνος ἐπήκουον τοῦ Πυθαγόρου μετὰ τοῦ καὶ βλέπειν αὐτόν, πρὸ τούτου δὲ ἐκτὸς αὐτῆς καὶ μηδέποτε αὐτῷ ἐνορῶντες μετεῖχον τῶν λόγων.

Parallel VI

Iamblichos 54	Justinus XX, 4, xvi	Iamblichos 50
Ταῖς δὲ γυναιξὶν .... περὶ τῆς πρὸς ἄνδρας ὁμιλίας κελεῦσαι κατανοεῖν .... καλῶς ἔχειν ἢ μηδὲν ἐναντιοῦσθαι πρὸς τοὺς ἄνδρας ἢ τότε νομίζειν νικᾶν ὅταν ἐκείνων ἡττηθῶσιν.	Matronarum quoque separatam a viris doctrinam et puerorum a parentibus habuit. Docebat nunc has pudicitiam et obsequia in viros,	Χωρὶς αὐτὸν [Πυθαγόραν] διαλεχθῆναι ἐν μὲν τῷ Πυθίῳ πρὸς τοὺς παῖδας, ἐν δὲ τῷ τῆς Ἥρας πρὸς τὰς γυναῖκας ἠξίωσαν [sc. οἱ Κροτωνιᾶται].
Iamblichos 37		
Περιχυθέντων δὲ τῶν νεανίσκων παραδέδοται λόγους τινας διαλεχθῆναι ἐξ ὧν εἰς τὴν σπουδὴν παρεκάλει πρὸς τοὺς γονέας.	nunc illos (sc. pueros) modestiam	
Iamblichos 42		
Παρεκάλει δὲ τοὺς νεανίσκους καὶ πρὸς τὴν παιδείαν	et studium literarum.	

fragments of Aristoxenos. Everywhere the original text has undergone a good deal of remolding, and this independence of the authors in using their source may have induced them to mingle the information derived from one source with that gained from others. Great caution must be used, therefore, in tracing these sources.

Let us now take up a single problem. Rohde[4] has contended that Justinus XX, 4—the chapter which deals with the history of Pythagoras and the Pythagoreans—is exclusively derived from Timaios, and his opinion has been universally accepted. Part of the evidence can be seen in the above parallels.[5] They show, to be sure, that there is only one very slight direct relation between a passage of Justinus and a fragment of Timaios.[6] But again and again a passage in Iamblichos that coincides in content with a fragment of Timaios is followed by a passage that resembles closely a passage in Justinus.[7] This is all the more significant because these latter passages are quite long while the whole chapter of Justinus is rather short.

Furthermore, if one does not confine the investigation to the immediate surroundings of the Iamblichos passages in question—which is perfectly legitimate since Justinus gives only an extract of the fuller account given by Pompeius Trogus—other observations of the same sort can be made.

In Parallel VI the similarity between Justinus and Iamblichos is close enough to suggest a common source, and since Iamblichos 37 closely follows[8] and Iamblichos 54 closely precedes[9] a passage in which Timaios is used, it is very likely that this common source is Timaios.

[4] *Op. cit.*, p. 133.
[5] II–IV.
[6] Parallel II.
[7] Parallels II and III.
[8] Cf. Parallel II.
[9] Cf. Parallel III.

In Parallel VII the coincidence with Porphyrios, who quotes Apollonios,[10] shows that Iamblichos copies this author, while Justinus seems to have drawn his information from the same source as Apollonios.

This gives all the more significance to a further coincidence between Iamblichos and Justinus, and a passage in Diogenes Laertios also, which is shown in Parallel VIII.

In this case Iamblichos himself says that he is quoting Apollonios, and again Justinus seems to give a summary of the account used by this author.

To this the observation may be added that in the course of these comparisons every single sentence in Justinus XX, 4 has found its equivalent in Iamblichos. The conclusion is therefore inevitable that Justinus, which means Pompeius Trogus, has made use of a single source throughout this part of his work, and that this same source has been largely, *though not necessarily exclusively*, used by Apollonios in the chapters borrowed by Iamblichos. As to the identification of this source, one may add to the evidence provided above that Trogus, as A. Enmann[11] has shown, must have made rather extensive use of the work of Timaios in all those parts of his history that deal with Sicily and Southern Italy.

Thus far the result is almost universally acknowledged. But it seemed necessary to put the evidence before the reader,[12] since it is impossible fully to understand the problems arising

[10] Compare also Iambl. 5 and Porph. 2. The resemblance between these two passages suggests that the use of Apollonios as a source by Iamblichos extends even further.

[11] *Ueber die Quellen der sicilischen Geschichte bei Pompeius Trogus* (Dorpat, 1880).

[12] Since the coincidences between the different authors have been discovered by different scholars, the evidence is scattered in a great many articles. I have therefore collected it and tried to arrange it so that all the interrelations may stand out as clearly as possible. I have also made a few minor additions of my own.

Parallel VII

Porphyrios 4	Iamblichos 11	Justinus XX, 4, iii
Διακοῦσαι δ᾽ οὐ μόνον Φερεκύδην ἀλλὰ καὶ Ἑρμοδάμαντα καὶ Ἀναξίμανδρόν φησιν οὗτος [sc. Apollonios].	[Πυθαγόρας] νύκτωρ λαβὼν πάντας μετὰ τοῦ Ἑρμοδάμαντος . . . . πρὸς τὸν Φερεκύδην διεπόρθμευσε καὶ πρὸς Ἀναξίμανδρον τὸν φυσικὸν καὶ πρὸς Θαλῆν εἰς Μίλητον.	Magnisque sapientiae incrementis ornatus

Iamblichos 19

Δύο δὴ καὶ εἴκοσι ἔτη κατὰ τὴν Αἴγυπτον ἐν τοῖς ἀδύτοις διετέλεσεν ἀστρονομιῶν καὶ γεωμετρῶν . . . ἕως ὑπὸ τῶν τοῦ Καμβύσου αἰχμαλωθεὶς εἰς Βαβυλῶνα ἀνήχθη καὶ ἐκεῖ τοῖς Μάγοις ἄσμενος ἀσμένοις συνδιατρίψας ἐκπαιδευθεὶς τὰ παρ᾽ αὐτοῖς . . . . ἄλλα τε δώδεκα ἔτη συνδιατρίψας εἰς Σάμον ὑπέστρεψε.

Aegyptum primo

mox *Babyloniam* ad perdiscendum siderum motus originemque mundi spectandam profectus summam scientiam consecutus est.

Parallel VIII

Iamblichos 254	Justinus XX, 4, xiv	Diogenes Laertios VIII, 3
Ἔπειτα καὶ τῶν νεανίσκων ὄντων ἐκ τῶν ἐν τοῖς ἀξιώμασι καὶ ταῖς οὐσίαις προεχόντων συνέβαινε .... μὴ μόνον αὐτοὺς ἐν τοῖς ἰδίοις οἴκους πρωτεύειν, ἀλλὰ κοινῇ τὴν πόλιν οἰκονομεῖν, μεγάλην μὲν ἑταιρείαν συναγηοχότας (ἦσαν γὰρ ὑπὲρ τριακοσίους)..... Ἐπεὶ δὲ.... κἀκεῖνος [sc. Πυθαγόρας] ἀπῆλθε, ἐξερράγη τὸ σιωπούμενον μῖσος.	Sed *CCC ex iuvenibus* cum sodalicii iure sacramento quodam nexi separatam a ceteris civibus vitam exercerent, quasi coetum clandestinae coniurationis haberent, civitatem in se converterunt.	[οἱ νεανίαι] πρὸς τοὺς τριακοσίους ὄντες ᾠκονόμουν τὰ πολιτικὰ ὥστε σχεδὸν ἀριστοκρατίαν εἶναι.

in the further course of the investigation without having the evidence constantly before one's eyes.

The assumption that the whole of Justinus XX, 4 is ultimately derived from Timaios implies that all the passages in Iamblichos which coincide with it have the same origin. Since, furthermore, Justinus gives only an abstract of the work of Trogus and since many of the chapters in Iamblichos in which coincidences with Justinus occur belong to fuller accounts which seem to be consistent and coherent in themselves, one is easily led to believe that these whole chapters are due to the same author in their entirety, excepting perhaps a few additions made by Apollonios that can be easily eliminated.

Starting from such considerations, Delatte (R)[13] has tried to prove that the whole quotation from Apollonios in Iamblichos 254-265 is derived from Timaios; Rostagni tried to show the same of Iamblichos 11-20, 25-29, 35, 54-56, 71-74, 75-79 (?), 80-81, and 170, and, though he does not say so *expressis verbis*, by implication he supposes the same of Iamblichos 133, 177, and some other chapters also. Bertermann, though differing from Rostagni in so far as he does not attribute Iamblichos 80-81 to Timaios but to Androkydes, an author of the second half of the fourth century who wrote Περὶ Πυθαγορικῶν συμβόλων has attributed still further passages in Iamblichos to the same source.

At this turn of the investigation, however, the difficulties begin. Let us start with a minor one.

In Chapter XX, 3 Justinus tells how the Krotonians suffered a terrible and unexpected defeat from the Locrians in the second half of the sixth century. Then (XX, 4, i) he proceeds: "*Post* haec Crotoniensibus nulla virtutis excercitatio, nulla armorum cura fuit. Oderant enim quae infeliciter sumpserant; mutassentque *vitam luxuria* ni Pythagoras philosophus fuisset." Following this Justinus first relates the

[13] See footnote 1 of this chapter.

life of Pythagoras up to his arrival at Kroton. Then he goes on: "Quibus omnibus instructus Crotonam venit populumque *in luxuriam lapsum* auctoritate sua ad frugalitatem revocavit." The chapter ends with the story of Pythagoras' migration from Kroton to Metapontum and of the catastrophe that befell the order after his death.

On account of the coincidence between part of this passage and part of the long quotation from Apollonios in Iamblichos 254[14] both Rostagni and Delatte agree that the whole of the account given by Iamblichos, so far as it refers to the same occurrences as Justinus XX, 4, xiv–xviii, is derived from the same source: Timaios. This account of Iamblichos runs as follows: συνέβαινε αὐτοὺς (sc. τοὺς τριακοσίους νεανίσκους) μὴ μόνον ἐν τοῖς ἰδίοις οἴκοις πρωτεύειν, ἀλλὰ κοινῇ τὴν πόλιν οἰκονομεῖν, μεγάλην μὲν ἑταιρείαν συναγηοχότας, μικρὸν δὲ μέρος τῆς πόλεως οὖσαν τῆς οὐκ ἐν τοῖς αὐτοῖς ἤθεσιν οὔτ' ἐπιτηδεύμασιν ἐκείνοις πολιτευομένης. Οὐ μὴν ἀλλὰ μέχρι μὲν οὖν τὴν ὑπάρχουσαν χώραν ἐκέκτηντο καὶ Πυθαγόρας ἐπεδήμει, διέμενεν ἡ μετὰ τὸν συνοικισμὸν κεχρονισμένη κατάστασις δυσαρεστουμένη καὶ ζητοῦσα καιρὸν μεταβολῆς. Ἐπεὶ δὲ Σύβαριν ἐχειρώσαντο καὶ ἐκεῖνος ἀπῆλθε καὶ τὴν δορύκτητον διῳκήσαντο μὴ κατακληρουχηθῆναι κατὰ τὴν ἐπιθυμίαν τῶν πολλῶν ἐξερράγη τὸ σιωπούμενον μῖσος καὶ διέστη πρὸς αὐτοὺς τὸ πλῆθος κτλ. As Rostagni pointed out, the only other passage in an ancient author in which the Pythagoreans are also connected with the conquest of Sybaris in any way is found in Diodoros XII, 9.[15] Since, for other reasons (as we shall see below), it is likely that Diodoros has made use of the work of Timaios in Books XI and XII, this seems to confirm the view that Iamblichos 254 is also derived from this author.

However, in Fragment 82 (= Athenaios XII, 22, 522) Timaios

---
[14] See Parallel VIII.
[15] The reference to Sybaris in Iambl. 133 and 177 is also derived from Apollonios and therefore does not represent independent evidence.

says: Καὶ Κροτωνιᾶται μετὰ τὸ ἐξελεῖν Σύβαριν ἐξώκειλαν εἰς τρυφήν, ὥστε καὶ τὸν ἄρχοντα αὐτῶν περιιέναι κατὰ τὴν πόλιν ἀλουργίδα ἠμφιεσμένον καὶ ἐστεφανωμένον χρυσῷ στεφάνῳ, ὑποδεδεμένον δὲ λευκὰς κρηπῖδας. In this fragment the τρυφή of the Krotonians is mentioned as following their victory over Sybaris, not their defeat in the war with Lokroi. Also, it seems rather difficult to insert the fragment into the story told by Iamblichos 254 ff.

Yet thus far one may still contend that Timaios may perhaps have spoken of two periods of τρυφή in Kroton, one preceding Pythagoras' arrival there, the other following his departure. In addition, the renewed inclination of the Krotonians towards luxury may have been represented as one of the motives in their rebellion against Pythagorean predominance. One may also point to the fact that τρυφή obviously played a large part in Timaios' conception of history,[16] and one may therefore consider the reference to the τρυφή of the Krotonians in Justinus XX, 4, i ff. as a confirmation of the assumption that this passage comes from Timaios. But it will be seen later that the interconnection of these passages has some bearing on other problems also.

The real difficulties begin as soon as one tries to reconstruct Timaios' chronology. Kothe, Delatte, Rostagni, Bertermann, though widely differing in their results, all start from the same premises. All of them have observed that there is some partial agreement between Iamblichos 19 and Justinus XX, 4, iii. All of them conclude that this points to a common source: Timaios. Hence, since the whole story told in Iamblichos 11–19 seems to be a unit, they all agree that this whole passage is Timean in origin.

These chapters contain a good amount of chronological data: (1) Pythagoras is 18 years of age when he leaves Samos

[16] Cf. Tim. Fr. 62: τρυφή of the inhabitants of Siris; Fr. 58-61: detailed description of the τρυφή of the Sybarites.

for the first time in order to study with Thales, Anaximander, and others. (2) Following this he spends 22 years in Egypt. (3) There follow 12 years in Babylonia. (4) Then he returns to Samos at the age of 56. Since 18+22+12 is only 52, one has to infer that he spent four years studying with Thales and the others. All this is very clear.

Kothe, Delatte, Rostagni, and Bertermann agree, further, in combining this with Iamblichos 265. Here we find that Pythagoras was head of the Pythagorean order for 39 years and that he died at an age of nearly 100. This, according to Synkellos I, 469 and Tzetzes XI, 22, means at the age of 99. Since 56+39 is 95, there are four or five more years to be accounted for. This is easy, since Iamblichos 20-28 tells us that Pythagoras, having returned from Babylonia, spent a few years in Samos, undertaking at the same time some shorter journeys to Crete, Sparta, and Delos. All this combined results in a wonderfully complete account of Pythagoras' whole life, and can be further supplemented by Justinus XX, 4, xvii who says that Pythagoras, having spent 20 years at Kroton, migrated to Metapontum. The 39 years during which he was the head of the order in Italy have, then, to be divided into 20 spent in Kroton and 19 in Metapontum. But how can this be converted into absolute chronology?

Rostagni starts from the assumption that Timaios dated the migration of Pythagoras in the year 529.[17] From this date the rest of the chronology can be easily derived. (See the table on facing page.)

This chronology, however, presents two serious difficulties. (1) Iamblichos 19 says that Pythagoras stayed 22 years in Egypt ἕως ὑπὸ τῶν τοῦ Καμβύσου αἰχμαλωθεὶς εἰς Βαβυλῶνα ἀνήχθη. This would fix the date of this event in the year 525 or 524, but according to Rostagni it should be dated in 545.

[17] *Op. cit.*, pp. 376 ff. His arguments in this case are rather cogent, though even here the conclusion is not absolutely certain.

CHRONOLOGY OF PYTHAGORAS' LIFE

59 years[19]		589	Birth of Pythagoras (529+4+56)
		571	Pythagoras leaves Samos at the age of 18[18]
		571–67	Travels and studies with Thales, etc. (4 years)
99 years[21]		567–45	Sojourn in Egypt (22 years)[20]
		545–33	Sojourn in Babylonia (12 years)[22]
		533–29	Second stay at Samos, journeys to Crete, Sparta, etc. (4 years)
39 years[24]		529–509	Pythagoras at Kroton (20 years)[23]
		509–490	Pythagoras at Metapontum (19 years)
		490	Death of Pythagoras

Rostagni therefore assumes that the words quoted above are to be eliminated as added by a later author, probably either Apollonios or Iamblichos. But one is perhaps justified in asking why just these few words should be removed if everything else is derived from Timaios. (2) The second difficulty is not mentioned by Rostagni. In Timaios Fragment 81 we read: Ἀκοῦσαι δ'αὐτὸν [sc. Ἐμπεδοκλέα] Πυθαγόρου Τίμαιος διὰ τῆς ἐνάτης ἱστορεῖ λέγων ὅτι καταγνωσθεὶς ἐπὶ λογοκλοπείᾳ τότε, καθὰ καὶ Πλάτων, τῶν λόγων ἐκωλύθη μετέχειν. It is scarcely possible that Empedokles, whose ἀκμή was dated in 444 by Apollodoros, whose grandfather won an Olympian victory in 496, and whose father played a leading part in Agrigentian politics in 470, should have "heard" Pythagoras, if Pythagoras died in 490.

Delatte[25] starts precisely with the two dates that cause the difficulty in Rostagni's chronology. Since, however, he would in this way make Pythagoras come to Kroton after the defeat

---

[18] Iambl. 11. [19] Iambl. 19. [20] *Ibid.*
[21] Synkellos. [22] *Ibid.* [23] Just. XX, 4.
[24] Iambl. 265. [25] *M*, pp. 5 ff.

and destruction of Sybaris, he reduces the duration of Pythagoras' second stay at Samos to one year and the length of his life to 95, contending that this is still "nearly 100" and that Synkellos and Tzetzes misunderstood Timaios' statement. But this scarcely reduces the difficulty. If Pythagoras went to Babylonia in 525, stayed there 12 years, then returned to Samos, and, another year having elapsed, migrated to Kroton, he still did not arrive there more than two years before the destruction of Sybaris. This is utterly irreconcilable with the story told by Justinus[26] and Timaios.[27] For, according to Justinus, Pythagoras came to Kroton when the Krotonians had fallen into τρυφή in their despair over the defeat suffered at the hands of the Lokrians. Through his teaching and influence he gradually succeeded in restoring frugality, simplicity, and strict moral principles, and finally their political strength. This later enabled them to defeat the Sybarites against heavy odds. According to Timaios[28] the Krotonians fell into τρυφή immediately following their victory. It is obvious that these two stories told in the same work, as Delatte assumes, are perfectly ridiculous if the interval between both events is supposed to be not more than two years.

Kothe,[29] it seems, was aware of this difficulty, for he dates the destruction of Sybaris to which Timaios Fragment 82 refers in the years between 478 and 467, making the assumption that Sybaris had been reconstructed in the meantime. But are we to assume that the great victory of 510 had no influence on the character of the Krotonians, but that the defeat of the miserable remnants of the Sybarites which may have occurred in the first half of the fifth century (as we shall see below), made them fall into τρυφή? And even if one con-

---

[26] XX, 4, i-xiii
[27] Fr. 82.
[28] *Ibid.*
[29] *Op. cit.*, p. 37.

sidered this as possible, there would still be the difficulty that the time from 512 to 510 is far too short to account for Justinus' story of the regenerating effect on the Krotonians of Pythagoras' teaching before their first great war with Sybaris. So all the reconstructions attempted so far encounter very serious difficulties.[30] Perhaps the error is to be found in their common premises.

In sections 20 and 21 Iamblichos tells us how Pythagoras returned to Samos after his stay in Babylonia. He is greatly honored by his fellow citizens and asked to let them partake of his wisdom. However, when he tries to introduce the Egyptian method of teaching through symbols, he finds no audience. So he hires a poor boy—also of the name of Pythagoras—whom he pays to attend his lectures until he becomes so enthusiastic that he not only attends them without pay, but is even willing to support Pythagoras from the proceeds of his manual labor, when Pythagoras pretends to have lost his wealth.

In this story the transition from the enthusiasm of the Samians for Pythagoras to their unwillingness to listen to him is rather sudden, but the author at least makes an attempt to explain it by Pythagoras' special method of teaching, and seems to say that Pythagoras did not succeed *in spite of* the fact that at first he aroused the admiration of his fellow citizens. At the end of this story, however, there is again a very sudden transition[31]: Τούτου δή (the younger Pythagoras) καὶ

---

[30] If there were no other way out of the difficulty, Rostagni's reconstruction would be preferable, since the passage about Kambyses *might*, after all, be a later addition; and the testimony of Tim. Fr. 81 *might* be explained away by the assumption that the author who quotes Timaios (Diog. Laert. VIII, 54) misunderstood an expression (ἀκουστὴς ἐγένετο) which meant merely that Empedokles was a Pythagorean ἀκουστής, not that he had been a pupil of Pythagoras personally. But the progress of our inquiry will show that the solution of the difficulty is different.

[31] Iambl. 25.

τὰ ἀλειπτικὰ συγγράμματα φέρεται . . . . οὐ καλῶς εἰς Πυθαγόραν τὸν Μνησάρχου τούτων ἀναφερομένων. λέγεται δὲ περὶ τὸν αὐτὸν χρόνον θαυμασθῆναι αὐτὸν περὶ τὴν Δῆλον κτλ. At first one is not even sure whether the sentence beginning with λέγεται refers to the younger Pythagoras or to the philosopher. Yet this might still be due to unintelligent compression of the original by Iamblichos. But as Apollonios goes on to tell how Pythagoras, having returned from his travels to Delos and other places, is greatly honored by the Samians and finally withdraws to Kroton because the honors and the civic duties connected with them are too much for him, it becomes increasingly clear that this is a continuation of the story told in the first part of Section 20, and that the story of his lack of success told in Section 20, ii-25, i is an insertion into the original context, taken from a different source. And if there is still some doubt in the mind of the reader, the author gives himself away completely when he concludes[32]: καὶ φεύγων τὰς πολιτικὰς ἀσχολίας, ὡς δ'ἔνιοι λέγουσι, τὴν περὶ παιδείας ὀλιγωρίαν τῶν τότε τὴν Σάμον οἰκούντων παραιτούμενος, ἀπῆρεν εἰς τὴν Ἰταλίαν κτλ. Here, then, he says himself that there existed two different versions, one of Pythagoras the successful, the other of Pythagoras the unsuccessful. But in the preceding chapters he has made an attempt to mold both versions into one story. This alone makes the one-source theory break down, and it is also revealing as to Apollonios' methods. But which, if either, of the two versions, is that of Timaios?

Let us compare the following passages:

[32] Iambl. 28.

TIMAIOS' VERSION

Iamblichos 11

Ὑποφυομένης δὲ ἄρτι τῆς Πολυκράτους τυραννίδος περὶ ὀκτωκαιδέκατον μάλιστα ἔτος γεγονὼς προορώμενός τε οἱ χωρήσει καὶ ὡς ἐμπόδιον ἔσται... τῇ ἀντὶ πάντων αὐτῷ σπουδαζομένῃ φ ι λ ο μ α θ ε ί ᾳ (sc. he went to Thales and later to *Egypt* and *Babylonia*).

Strabo XIV, 638

Ἐπὶ τούτου (sc. Π ο λ υ κ ρ ά τ ο υ s) δὲ καὶ Πυθαγόραν ἱστοροῦσι ἰδόντα φυομένην τ ὴ ν τ υ ρ α ν ν ί δ α ἐκλιπεῖν τὴν πόλιν καὶ ἀπελθεῖν εἰς Α ἴ - γ υ π τ ο ν καὶ Β α β υ λ ῶ ν α φ ι λ ο - μ α θ ε ί α s χάριν.

Iamblichos 28

Ὑπὸ τῶν αὐτοῦ πολιτῶν εἰς τὰς πρεσβείας πάσας ἑλκόμενος καὶ μετέχειν ἀναγκαζόμενος τῶν αὐτῶν λειτουργιῶν καὶ συνιδὼν ὅτι τοὺς τῆς πατρίδος νόμους πειθόμενον χαλεπὸν αὐτοῦ μένοντα φιλοσοφεῖν καὶ διότι πάντες οἱ πρότερον φιλοσοφήσαντες ἐπὶ ξένης τὸν βίον διετέλεσαν (sic!)......
ἀπῆρεν εἰς τὴν Ἰταλίαν.

ἐπανιόντα δ' ἐκεῖθεν ὁρῶντα ἔτι συμμένουσαν τὴν τυραννίδα πλεύσαντα εἰς Ἰταλίαν ἐκεῖ διατελέσαι τὸν βίον.

On account of the similarity in the wording, there can be no doubt that Iamblichos 11 and Strabo XIV, 638 are derived from the same source; and the other coincidences discussed above make it very likely indeed that this common source is Timaios. But the story ends quite differently in Iamblichos 28 and in Strabo. Both the versions found in Iamblichos 20-28 presuppose that tyranny has ceased to exist in Samos when Pythagoras returns, while according to Strabo he leaves again for the very reason that he finds tyranny still in force.

This is very significant, for as long as the duration of Pythagoras' journeys to Egypt and Babylonia is not determined, Strabo's story is quite unobjectionable. Polykrates was killed between 523 and 521. His first accession to power, together with his two brothers Pantognotos and Syloson, can scarcely be dated much before 540, certainly not before or even in the time of the war between Samos and Priene. But the interval between those two dates leaves ample time for Pythagoras' journeys to Egypt and Babylonia. If, however, the further assumption is made that he spent 22 years in Egypt and 12 years in Babylonia, Strabo's version becomes chronologically untenable. For this would presuppose that Pythagoras already saw tyranny approaching in 571.[33] The addition of these dates, therefore, is tantamount to making him return under a different regime. This agrees with the version of Apollonios.

Which one of the two, then, has preserved the original version? There is obviously no reason why Strabo should have changed the story if he found it in the form in which it is given by Iamblichos. Also it is very unlikely in itself that, in so short and incidental an account as he is giving, he should have mixed two different sources—quite apart from the fact that this is not his usual method.

Apollonios, on the other hand, had every reason to change the original story after having inserted the chronological data found in Iamblichos 19 since these would otherwise upset the chronology. He has already been found to have mingled different sources in these very chapters. Thus he has the motive. He has been convicted of similar crimes, and he betrays his bad conscience by finishing his account with a rather muddled and inconsistent story. There can be scarcely any doubt that he is the criminal.

If this is acknowledged—and I do not see how it can be contested when it is once pointed out—it becomes clear that the chronological data in Iamblichos 19 do not belong to the common source of Apollonios, Justinus, and Strabo, but are a

[33] It is obvious that the words of Strabo ὁρῶντα ἔτι συμμένουσαν τὴν τυραννίδα refer neither to the troubles under Maiandrios nor to the time of Persian supremacy, and that such an assumption would not solve the chronological difficulty.

later invention. If this is so, the common foundation of the reconstructions attempted by Rostagni, Bertermann, Delatte and Kothe breaks down.

Thus far, the result is negative. Let us consider what parts of their findings may be still used to advantage. (1) It is still very probable that Justinus XX, 4 is derived from Timaios exclusively. The passage can still be used in a further investigation into the sources. (2) The arguments of Rostagni in favor of his assumption that Timaios dated the migration of Pythagoras to Kroton in 529 have not lost their strength, and the seeming evidence to the contrary has disappeared with his already rejected conclusions. (3) Timaios Fragment 81 still makes it very probable that Timaios dated the death of Pythagoras rather late, probably not before 470, though in this respect there is no certainty. (4) Delatte's reconstruction is still valid as a reconstruction of Apollonios' chronology, though not of that of Timaios. (5) It has been proved beyond doubt that Apollonios sometimes makes up his story from different sources in a rather arbitrary way. But there is also no doubt that he *has* made use of very valuable material, and it is extremely likely that in some cases his ultimate source is Timaios. This much will provide a starting point for our further investigation.

The most important chapter concerned with the history of the Pythagoreans in Iamblichos that has not yet been discussed is the extract from Apollonios in Sections 254 ff. That there is a striking coincidence between Iamblichos 254 and Justinus XX, 4, xiv has already been mentioned.[34] There is some agreement between Iamblichos 263 and Polybios II, 39, iv in the fact that both passages allude to interference of the Achaeans in Pythagorean affairs at Kroton.[35] There is some connection between Iamblichos 254 and Diodoros XII, 9, in

[34] Cf. p. 46.
[35] This fact is not mentioned by any other author except Strabo, who gives merely an abstract of Polybios' version.

so far as both authors say that the Pythagoreans had something to do with the conflict between Kroton and Sybaris. In this case the connection is very slight, since Diodoros tells us that Pythagoras played a part in bringing about the downfall of Sybaris, while Iamblichos says that the events that followed the conquest of Sybaris led to the destruction of the Pythagorean order. However, Julius Beloch[36] has pointed out that the repetition of the history of Sybaris at the time when the foundation of her successor-city is about to be told is typical of Timaios. In addition, Diodoros mentions the incredible figure of 300,000 Sybarites who are supposed to have fought 100,000 Krotonians, and Iamblichos casually refers to the same figure in the speech which he puts in the mouth of the demagogue Ninon.

It is therefore certain that Apollonios derived part of his story from rather early sources, and it is very likely that one of them is Timaios. But again one has to be very careful not to draw rash conclusions. Delatte[37] has tried to prove that the whole extract from Apollonios is derived from Timaios exclusively. His arguments are as follows: (1) The coincidences with Polybios, Justinus, and Diodoros. (2) The style of the extract, which seems more sober and matter of fact than the rest of the work of Apollonios. (3) The appearance in this extract of the Pythagorean troubles as only a part of a larger struggle between aristocratic and democratic forces in Southern Italy—this seems the view of a writer of general history rather than of a specialist in Pythagoreanism. (4) The contradiction between the account given in this passage and other passages in Iamblichos that are also derived from Apollonios. In Iamblichos 29, for instance, we are told that 600 men joined the order, while in Section 254 we read of only 300. In

[36] *Neue Jahrbücher für klassische Philologie und Jugendbildung*, CXXIII, 699.
[37] *R*, pp. 90 ff.

Section 72 we are told that there were different groups among the Pythagoreans, one of them the πολιτικοί, in Section 254 we hear of πολιτικοί only. (5) The unity of the whole story told in Sections 254-263—it cannot be split up into parts derived from different sources. (6) The mention in Section 263 of Deinarchos and Litages as if they were known to the reader, though no mention of them has been made before. This seems to indicate that Apollonios gives an abstract of a fuller account.

Let us examine these arguments briefly. (6) Deinarchos and Litages are the leaders of the same conflicting parties that are mentioned in 257. In that paragraph we find the names of Deimachos and Theages as those of leaders of these parties. It is obvious that the difference is due to a mistake of the copyists,[38] possibly of Iamblichos himself, since errors of this kind are very frequent in his work.[39] And even if this were not true, the shortening would have to be ascribed to Iamblichos, not to Apollonios, who is much more apt to enlarge the accounts found in his authorities. (5) As to the unity of the passage one has only to point to the fact that it is a custom of Apollonios to mold different versions into one story, so that they seemingly form a unit. (4) He may have found a way even to reconcile the story of 600 *followers* of Pythagoras in Section 72 with that of 300 νεανίσκοι in Section 254. (3) The observation that Iamblichos 254 ff. are written from the point of view of a writer of general history is excellent. This observation, which cannot be contested, proves that Apollonios has been greatly influenced by such an author in the whole composition of this part of his work. But it does not prove that he has made use of this author exclusively. The same applies to the first and second argument.

[38] In this case the corruption of Δεινάρχου into Δειμάχου is easily explained by the fact that the name is preceded by 'Αλκιμάχου.
[39] Cf., for instance, *Theokles* (130), *Theaitetos* (173), *Euthykles* (267), all the same person.

The observations, however, on which these arguments are based can be used in the further inquiry. (1) Rostagni has drawn attention to the fact that Justinus XX, 4, xvi says that 60 Pythagoreans perished in the burning house at Kroton, while Apollonios in Iamblichos 263 states that 60 Pythagoreans returned from exile when a settlement had been brought about. Rostagni thought that this coincidence of figures points also to a common source. But if this is the case, it shows at the same time that Apollonios has made a very arbitrary use of his material. (2) The sober style which Delatte considered as an indication of a special source is not found everywhere in this extract, certainly not in the speech of the demagogue Ninon in Sections 258 f. This passage is also interesting in many other respects. Rohde[40] has pointed out that the speech itself is composed of bits of genuine tradition on Pythagorean doctrine, but that these are put together very arbitrarily. In the same speech the Pythagoreans are accused of tyrannical as well as oligarchic tendencies. Yet at the epoch in question tyrants usually were supported by the lower classes, and the aristocrats were their most fervent opponents. It is only with the rise of radical oligarchic tendencies and doctrines in Athens in the second half of the fifth century that the notions of oligarch and tyrant become confounded, a fact which can scarcely have been unknown to Timaios.

The same inconsistency is even more patent in other passages of this part of Apollonios' account. In Section 257 the *Pythagoreans* Alkimachos, Deimachos, Meton, and Demokedes urge the people to uphold the πάτριος πολιτεία. Yet, whether in Section 257 the χρόνων of the manuscripts, which does not make sense, is to be replaced by χιλίων with Delatte or by ἀρχόντων with Rostagni, the whole context shows that the opponents of the Pythagoreans belong to the governing

[40] *Op. cit.*, II, 134.

body of the city. What is more, the Pythagoreans, according to Section 254—and here Apollonios agrees with Justinus XX, 4, xiv—are those who introduce new types of political clubs and on the whole, appear as political innovators. One would therefore rather suppose that the opponents of the Pythagoreans are the defenders of the πάτριος πολιτεία. This view is confirmed by the fact that among them there is a speaker for the wealthy and a speaker for the δῆμος. It seems therefore that two different explanations of these events are confounded in Apollonios' account, one according to which the Pythagoreans were attacked by both the ruling parties because of the suspicion aroused by the secrecy of their meetings, the strangeness of their doctrines, and their attempt to gain political influence, another according to which they were attacked by the democrats on account of their aristocratic leanings.

There are, however, traces of still another version. One of the leaders of the opponents of the Pythagoreans in Apollonios' account bears the name of Hippasos, the famous mathematician who was punished by the gods because he made public the theory of irrationals which had been kept secret by the Pythagoreans, and who in Iamblichos 81 appears as the founder of the group of the ἀκουσματικοί. This induced P. Tannery[41] to make the assumption that the real cause of the political conflict was a split in the Pythagorean order itself. His view is rightly rejected by Delatte[42] in so far as this is certainly not the predominating version of the event in the account given by Apollonios. Yet Tannery's observation must not be neglected. There are some curious coincidences between Iamblichos 264 and 88 where the split in the order and its division into the groups of the μαθηματικοί and the ἀκουσματικοί is discussed. In Iamblichos 264 Apollonios says that the πρεσβύτεροι who were interested in

[41] *Archiv für Geschichte der Philosophie*, I, 28–36.
[42] *B*, p. 244.

medicine were the leaders of the Pythagoreans when they returned to Kroton. This agrees with Iamblichos 88, where we are told that the πρεσβύτεροι were the political leaders of the order, in contrast with Section 254, where the νεανίσκοι are the politicians among the Pythagoreans. Also, in Section 88 one finds a simile taken from *medicine*.

Here, then, we find some traces of another version, the origin of which can still be traced to some extent. For the passage on the μαθηματικοί and ἀκουσματικοί in Iamblichos 81 and 88 can be traced to Nikomachos and, possibly, further to Androkydes.[43]

Furthermore, since Kylon is made to play a leading part in the political disturbances, Aristoxenos' version may also have influenced Apollonios' story,[44] though not necessarily directly.

As to the first and second explanations of the events traced in the present analysis, it would be easier to identify the sources if there existed a piece of independent tradition comparable to the one found in Strabo which referred to the story of Pythagoras' second stay in Samos.[45] It is quite possible and even likely that both these explanations had already been combined by Timaios. For Justinus—and there is still no reason to doubt that his account derives mainly from Timaios —says that the secrecy of the activities of the Pythagoreans and their separation from the rest of the people caused resentment among all classes of the citizens. On the other hand, it is likely on general grounds[46] that the broad historical view which saw in the Pythagorean disturbances only a part of a larger struggle between aristocratic and democratic forces is that of Timaios. There may have been general resentment

[43] Cf. p. 45; see Bertermann, *op. cit.* (p. 3, footnote 1), p. 19.
[44] Cf. pp. 11, 31.
[45] Cf. p. 53.
[46] Cf. p. 56; Polybios II, 39, ii–vi, indeed, seems to hint at something of the kind.

against Pythagorean austerity as well as against the mystery surrounding their activities in the time of triumph following the conquest of Sybaris, as suggested by Justinus and Timaios Fragment 82. This resentment, while still playing a great part in the feeling of the people in a later period, may have assumed a different character at a time when the Pythagoreans appeared as the defenders of old aristocratic principles against rising democratic tendencies. But it is scarcely credible that Timaios should have represented the Pythagoreans as defending the πάτριος πολιτεία not only *against the actual rulers* of the city but against both the dominant parties, much less that he should have mixed together all the different explanations, traces of which are found in the account of Apollodoros.

But why—one may perhaps ask—should Apollonios have made up such a confused story? Why should he not, at least, have kept separate those parts of the story which he found separated in Timaios? He might still have inserted other bits of information which he found in Nikomachos and other sources. The answer to this question can probably be found in his predilection for what might almost be called large-scale historical fresco painting. It is perhaps not unimportant to note that all the great names of Pythagoreans and Krotonians of the last years of the sixth and the first half of the fifth century enter into his account. There is the name of Demokedes,[47] the Krotonian physician,[48] who was already famous when he was called to the court of Polykrates of Samos[49] and who, after having spent some years at the Persian court, later escaped to his home country. There is the name of the great mathematician Hippasos,[50] who founded the group of the

[47] Herodotos III, 129-138; Athenaios XII, 22, p. 522 b.
[48] Notice also the references to medicine in Iambl. 264.
[49] Notice that Polykrates was killed in 522.
[50] Notice that Hippasos is referred to in other parts of Apollonios' work in such a way that there can be no doubt as to his identity.

ἀκουσματικοί and was the first to bring Pythagorean secrets before the public. There is Theages, who was later supposed to have written a treatise περὶ ἀρετῆς.[51] There is, of course, Kylon. There is Ninon, whose name had become proverbial through the saying οὐ τάδε ἐπὶ Νίνωνος, and who may have been mentioned by Timaios for that very reason.[52] All these famous names and the names of certain less well known persons are united in one great historical scene. Yet, if Demokedes was the physician of Polykrates and Dareios, if Kylon was expelled from the order while Pythagoras was still living at Kroton, as all the other authors say, and if Hippasos is the mathematician who discovered incommensurability, a discovery that can scarcely have been made before the middle of the fifth century, they cannot have been politically active at the same time. For the difficulty cannot be avoided by the assumption that Hippasos became a political leader when he was very young and made his mathematical discoveries in his old age, since his conflict with the Pythagoreans is supposed to have originated from this very discovery.

This discrepancy in Apollonios' chronology can be illustrated by some further observations. The introduction to his account suggests that the downfall of the Pythagoreans at Kroton occurred not so very long after the conquest of Sybaris and during the lifetime of Pythagoras, though after his migration to Metapontum.[53] This agrees to some extent with the end of his story, where he says[54] that ἐπιγιγνομένων πολλῶν ἐτῶν, when the leaders of the conflicting parties had died, the Pythagoreans were allowed to return to Kroton and henceforth were held in great honor. For this sentence seems to

[51] Cf. Stobaios, Floril. I, 117 ff.
[52] Rostagni has pointed out that this must really have been an old saying, since Aristophanes (Ekkl. 943) jokingly refers to it: οὐ γὰρ τἀπὶ Χαριξένης τάδ' ἐστι.
[53] Section 255.
[54] Section 263.

TIMAIOS' VERSION 63

indicate that the Pythagoreans returned after a long period of exile. Yet, a little later he implies that not only the younger ones from among the former leaders returned, but also some of the πρεσβύτεροι, which seems to show that the πολλὰ ἔτη mean a period of moderate length; and the chronological discrepancy becomes patent when, still a little further on, Apollonios says that οἱ σωθέντες (sc. from the catastrophe at Kroton) were killed while fighting for Kroton against the Thurians. For, however one may stretch the chronology, it is impossible to assume that persons who were adults and played a part in politics not very long after the destruction of Sybaris in 510 were still able to fight in a battle against the citizens of Thurioi, which city was founded in 444.

This is all the more remarkable because no such discrepancy can be found in the account given by Polybios,[55] which otherwise coincides with Apollonios' story in a good many details. Polybios does not mention any dates, but the causal connection of the events as they are reported by him makes it necessary to assume that the general unrest in Southern Italy followed immediately upon the destruction of the Pythagorean order, and that the interval between the beginning of this general revolution and the settlement brought about with the help of the Achaeans was not so very long. According to Polybios, then, the πολλὰ ἔτη of Apollonios were a comparatively short period. This does not cause any difficulty in his account, since he obviously does not date the anti-Pythagorean rebellion far back in the beginning of the fifth century.

[55] II, 39, 148–149: καθ' οὓς καιροὺς ἐν τοῖς κατὰ τὴν Ἰταλίαν τόποις κατὰ τὴν Μεγάλην Ἑλλάδα τότε προσαγορευομένην ἐνεπρήσθη τὰ συνέδρια τῶν Πυθαγορείων μετὰ ταῦτα γενομένου ὁλοσχεροῦς κινήματος περὶ τὰς πολιτείας ὅπερ εἰκὸς ὡς ἂν τῶν πρώτων ἐξ ἑκάστης πόλεως οὕτω παραλόγως διαφθαρέντων συνέβη τὰς κατ' ἐκείνους τοὺς τόπους Ἑλληνικὰς πόλεις ἀναπλησθῆναι φόνου καὶ στάσεως καὶ παντοδαπῆς ταραχῆς. Ἐν οἷς καιροῖς ἀπὸ τῶν πλείστων μερῶν τῆς Ἑλλάδος πρεσβευόντων ἐπὶ τὰς διαλύσεις Ἀχαιοῖς καὶ τῇ τούτων πίστει συνεχρήσαντο πρὸς τὴν τῶν παρόντων κακῶν ἐξαγωγήν.

So we obtain the final proof that Apollonios did not follow one single authority in this part of his work, as Delatte believed, but made up his story in a rather arbitrary fashion from the information found in different earlier works. We see also very clearly that the chronological confusion which is so patent in his work does not belong to that source which he has in common with Polybios. For Polybios' account is entirely consistent and clear, while that of Apollonios is not; and again the reason of the difference stands out very clearly.

It is quite in the character of Apollonios that he wanted to unite all the famous names of early fifth-century Kroton in one great historical picture. Kylon, one of the most outstanding figures of the epoch, was firmly dated in the lifetime of Pythagoras. Even Aristoxenos did not dare to give up this synchronism though it created some difficulty in his chronology. So Apollonios, if he wanted to make use of the person of Kylon in his story of the downfall of the Pythagorean rule, had to date this event in the early part of the fifth century. He obviously tried to make a kind of chronological adjustment by inserting the words ἐπιγιγνομένων δὲ πολλῶν ἐτῶν. But this did not really eliminate the chronological difficulty. It seems therefore that Apollonios sacrificed complete chronological consistency for the desire to draw a wonderful historical picture and that he used all the available material in a rather arbitrary fashion to make this picture more colorful. This is not very different from the way in which, in the passage Iamblichos 19–28, he changed the story found in his source in order to bring in all the figures that he could find. For in that case too it is the very abundance—in this case of chronological data—which causes chronological difficulties.

All this, however, by no means makes his account worthless as a source of historical information. When the chronological difficulty is removed by explaining the insertion of a great many names in one historical scene, his story is no longer at variance with the version of Aristoxenos, who dates the Krotonian catastrophe in the lifetime of Lysis, the teacher of Epaminondas. The coincidence between Apollonios and Polybios in their references to a settlement brought about by the mediation of the Achaeans points to a common source. This coincidence is all the more important because Apollonios[56] refers to documentary evidence and since Polybios[57] says that Timaios was especially anxious to support his statements by evidence of this sort. It is then extremely probable that this part of Apollonios' story is derived from Timaios, and if this is the case, the other parts of his account, as far as they do not give colorful details but discuss the general character of the Pythagorean rule in the light of the universal history of the period, are in all likelihood derived from the same source.

Let us, then, briefly sum up the results of this part of the investigation. The contents of the fragments collected in the different parallels above can be traced back to Timaios with certainty, though the original wording is scarcely ever preserved. This is not true of the many passages quoted by Iamblichos from the work of Apollonios which Rostagni, Delatte, and Bertermann have assigned to the same source. Many parts of these fragments have to be eliminated as fanciful additions by Apollonios himself. But when this has been done, there still remains quite a considerable and recognizable amount which can be attributed to Timaios with great probability. Finally, it is extremely likely that Polybios derived his account of the history of the Pythagoreans mainly, if not exclusively, from the same source.

But what were the sources of Timaios' knowledge and what can we know of their reliability? Twice there is some hint at documentary evidence. Κροτωνιατῶν ὑπομνήματα are men-

[56] Iambl. 262: ὡς ἐν τοῖς τῶν Κροτωνιατῶν ὑπομνήμασιν ἀναγέγραπται.
[57] XII, 10, iv; cf. also XII, 9, iii; XII, 10, ix; and *passim*.

tioned[58] and ὅρκοι which were deposited at Delphi.[59] We cannot test this evidence. The ὑπομνήματα may have been contained in a local chronicle which might have been embellished by legends, and we do not know whether Timaios ever saw the ὅρκοι. Yet the first half of the fifth century is the time when some kind of official records began to be kept in all the more important Greek cities, and in those cities there must have been available to him at least lists of the leading magistrates, from which important conclusions could be drawn.

Polybios blamed Timaios because he was a "Stubengelehrter" and lacked the historical insight which only a man who had himself been an active statesman could possess. This may have been a handicap in his evaluation of the character of the Pythagorean "rule" but scarcely to such an extent as to make him incapable of determining whether the Pythagoreans as such were the official rulers of the cities concerned or not. It certainly cannot have impaired his reliability in questions of chronology and the like.

Timaios had not the firsthand information which Aristoxenos obtained from the last Pythagoreans. But on the other hand there is no trace in his work of any bias either against or in favor of the Pythagoreans such as Aristoxenos so conspicuously displays. But what is most important: over both Dikaiarchos and Aristoxenos he has the enormous advantage that he deals with the Pythagoreans within the framework of a general history of Southern Italy so that he has to correlate and check in all directions.

For this reason it is a very great pity that no ancient author who has made use of the work of Timaios or preserved fragments of it gives us the slightest hint as to the absolute chronology of the history of the Pythagorean order after the death of Pythagoras which Timaios' work must have

[58] Iambl. 262.
[59] Iambl. 263.

contained. It will therefore be our next task to make an attempt to reconstruct this chronology. In doing this we shall have to avail ourselves of exactly the same means as Timaios himself: inferences that can be drawn from the general history of Southern Italy, Sicily, and Greece, and the documentary evidence, which—in the absence of relevant inscriptions —is in the main numismatic.

CHAPTER IV

The Chronological Questions and the Numismatic Evidence

BEFORE entering upon the discussion of the political history of the Pythagoreans as such some problems concerning the history of Kroton and Sybaris (including its successor city Thurioi) will have to be discussed.

Dionysios of Halikarnassos[1] says that Kleinias, the tyrant of the Krotonians, succeeded in robbing many towns of Southern Italy of their freedom with the help of exiles and slaves whom he had set free, and that he also banished and killed many noble Krotonians. Since Dionysios immediately afterwards speaks of Anaxilas (494–476), it would seem that he considered Kleinias as his contemporary.

Diodoros[2] states that Hieron, when he became suspicious of the popularity of his brother Polyzelos, decided to get rid of him in some convenient fashion. Therefore, when the Sybarites, who at that time were beleaguered by the Krotonians, asked for his aid, he sent his brother with a mercenary army, hoping that he would be killed while fighting the superior forces of the Krotonians. If this is more than a legend,[3] it

[1] *Antiquitates Romanae* XX, 7.
[2] XI, 48, iii.
[3] Schol. Pindar. *Olymp.* II, 29 and 37, tells the same story, but with the variation that Polyzelos is sent *against* the Sybarites.

suggests that at that time (476) Sybaris had been restored, though the Sybarites *might* have been beleaguered in some other stronghold of theirs where they had gathered after the destruction of their city in 510. In any case, if there was a restoration, it cannot have amounted to very much. For in 453 the city had again to be restored, and Diodoros,[4] when telling of this event, says that it took place 58 years after the destruction of the city, not mentioning any former restoration.

Let us then turn to the events of the second half of the fifth century.

1. According to Diodoros[5] Sybaris was restored in 453, but again destroyed by the Krotonians five years later in 448.

2. As to the foundation of Thurioi, Diodoros[6] places this among the events of the year 446, while other authors[7] date it in the 12th year before the outbreak of the Peloponnesian War, or the 16th year of the life of Lysias, whose birth is placed by the same authors in Olympiad 80, 2 (459 B.C.). This would date the foundation of Thurioi in 445/4. Furthermore, Diodoros X, 9 implies that the city received the name of Thurioi immediately upon its foundation, but says later[8] that after some time the Sybarites who had taken part in the foundation of the new city were driven out because they claimed supremacy over the rest of the citizens who had come from other places. This must be combined with Diodoros XII, 22, according to which passage the Sybarites who escaped from the civil strife founded a new city on the Traeis.[9] According to the *Vita decem oratorum*, on the other hand, the new city, founded in 444, was first called Sybaris and its name was later changed to Thurioi.

[4] XI, 90.
[5] XI, 90 and X, 10.
[6] X, 9-10.
[7] *Vita decem oratorum: Lysias* 835d; Dion. Hal. Περὶ τῶν ἀρχαίων ῥητόρων 452.
[8] XII, 11.
[9] Cf. also Strabo VI, 14, p. 263.

The question has been much discussed.[10] That there was a change in the name of the city is proved by the coins. There are (1) coins with the inscription ΣΥBA, with the head of Athena on one side and the bull of Sybaris (with the head turned back) on the other.[11] (2) Coins with the inscription ΣΥBAPI, with the head of Athena on one side and the bull of Thurioi (with the head turned forward and a fish beneath his feet) on the other side.[12] (3) Coins with the inscription ΘΟΥΡΙΩΝ and the same symbols as (2).[13]

Since Sybaris on the Traeis, which was founded after the quarrel with the other settlers, including the Athenians, would certainly not have put the head of Athena on its coins, these coins provide us with absolutely conclusive evidence that the colony which later received the name of Thurioi had first been called Sybaris. The fact that there are three different types of coins indicates that, following the exodus of the Sybarites, the symbol of the town was first changed, and only some time later its name. Since all the coins of type (1) and (2) and some of the coins of type (3) are of the same style,[14]

[10] A full discussion of the earlier literature is to be found in: Georg Busolt, *Griechische Geschichte*, Vol. III, Part 1, p. 523, note 2; cf. also Julius Beloch, *Griechische Geschichte*, Vol. II, Part 1, p. 200, note 4, and E. Ciaceri, *Storia della Magna Grecia*, II, 346.

[11] S. W. Grose, *Catalogue of the Fitzwilliam Museum*, I, Pl. XXXVIII, 28 and 29.

[12] S. W. Grose, *Catalogue of the Fitzwilliam Museum*, I, Pl. XXXVIII, 27; cf. also *Catalogue of Greek Coins of the British Museum, Italy*, p. 286 (Lucania, No. 32), and *The Cambridge Ancient History*, Volume of Plates II, 4, b.

[13] S. W. Grose, *Catalogue of the Fitzwilliam Museum*, I, Pl. XXXIX; F. E. Adcock in *The Cambridge Ancient History*, V, 168, note 2, mentions type (1) and type (3) only, but the coin in Volume of Plates II, 4, b, to which he refers as to an example of type (1), is really an example of type (2).

[14] J. Beloch (*op. cit.*, II, 1, 200, note 4) quotes A. Furtwaengler, *Meisterwerke der griechischen Plastik*, pp. 144 ff. as saying that the coins of type (3) show a more developed style than those of type (1). But

the changes must have succeeded one another rather rapidly. Whether this is to be explained by the assumption that the first foundation of the colony took place in 446, as suggested by Diodoros XII, 9, and that the name was changed and new settlers were called in[15] in 444 (the date of the foundation according to the *Vita decem oratorum* and the chronographers[16]), or whether we must assume a chronological error in Diodoros' account is not absolutely certain. But this second assumption is no longer necessary, and it is certain that only a very short time can have elapsed between the foundation of the colony and its renaming. Yet there was an intermediate time during which the colony still kept the name of Sybaris though the Sybarites had been driven out and the symbol of the city changed. This may have made it possible for some people still to call the city by its old name even for some time after the renaming had officially taken place. This is probably the case with Herodotos, who mentions the Sybarites of his own time in a passage[17] that can scarcely have been written before his stay in Athens in 443, and yet cannot refer to Sybaris on the Traeis.

3. Soon after the second settlement[18] there seems to have

Furtwaengler does not say so, and such a statement would not correspond to the facts. For though there are coins of type (3) that are of a more advanced style than those of type (1) and (2), there are others of exactly the same style. This is also stated by Furtwaengler. Beloch's conclusion, therefore, that several years must have elapsed between the foundation of the colony and its renaming does not hold.

[15] Diodoros XII, 11.
[16] In this case Diodoros would have committed the error of assuming that the colony got the name of Thurioi at once, and the *Vita decem oratorum* would be wrong in the statement that the name was changed *after* 444.
[17] V, 45.
[18] According to Diod. XII, 23 in Ol. 84, 1 (444 B.C.); that is, in the very same year.

broken out a long war between Thurioi and Tarentum[19] that ended only some time before the foundation of Herakleia by Tarentum in 433.[20]

4. Diodoros[21] relates further that in 434-33 a dispute again arose among the citizens of Thurioi as to who should be considered as the founder of the city. It was settled by an oracle from Delphi which declared the god himself to be the founder.

After this survey of certain facts related by ancient authors without direct reference to the history of the Pythagoreans, let us return to an analysis of Polybios II, 39 and Apollonios. Polybios gives the following account: (1) The συνέδρια of the Pythagoreans are burnt all over Southern Italy. (2) This is immediately followed by a κίνημα ὁλοσχερές throughout the region, with civil war, disorder, and slaughter everywhere. These disturbances are explained as a natural consequence of the fact that *the leading personalities in all the important cities had perished in the attack upon the Pythagoreans*. (3) On account of these troubles embassies arrive from all parts of the Greek motherland. Under the leadership of the Achaeans they bring about a peaceful settlement. (4) Still some time later (ἀλλὰ μετά τινας χρόνους) the cities of Southern Italy begin to imitate the Achaean institutions in detail. Kroton, Sybaris, and Kaulonia call in the Achaeans again, conclude an alliance with one another, and consecrate a sanctuary of Zeus Homarios—obviously in imitation of the old Homarion near Helike in Achaia—where they are going to have their common meetings. Though Polybios does not say so in so many words, he obviously implies that there gradually developed in Southern Italy something similar to the Achaean confederacy in the motherland. He further says that the Greek cities in Southern Italy imitated the customs and institutions

[19] Cf. also Antiochos in Strabo VI, 264.
[20] Cf. Strabo VI, 264 and Diodoros XII, 36.
[21] XI, 35.

of the Achaeans and implies that they adopted the principles of democratic government. (5) Finally, however, Dionysios and the Lucanians compelled them to give up both their confederacy and their democratic institutions.

This last event is the only one that can be easily and precisely dated. For it was in 388 that Dionysios the elder subjugated Rhegion and Kaulonia and put an end to Krotonian influence in Southern Italy. As to the rest of Polybios' story no precise dates can be established. However, Polybios represents the process of the democratization of Southern Italy and of the adoption of Achaean principles as a slow and gradual one. Nor does he say that the overthrow of democratic institutions under the pressure of Dionysios occurred immediately, or even rather soon, after their adoption. On the contrary, his account suggests that there elapsed a considerable time between the two events. As Unger[22] has pointed out, the Spartans established an oligarchic regime in Achaia in 417.[23] The democratic influence of the Achaeans in Southern Italy, therefore, must have been exercised before that time. There is perhaps an even earlier *terminus ante quem*. The great peace conference and settlement of Sicilian affairs at Gela in 424 was brought about not through mediation by the Greeks of the continent, but through the desire of the Sicilian cities to defend themselves against the constant meddling in their affairs of the warring tribes and states of the motherland. And though this conference dealt mainly with Sicilian affairs, it shows very clearly that the time of the Peloponnesian War was not the period in which the Greeks of the motherland were likely to bring about a pacific settlement in Italy. It is therefore very likely that the mediation of the Achaeans took place some time before the Peloponnesian War, probably somewhere near the time of the foundation of Thurioi, in which

[22] *Op. cit.* (p. 3, footnote 1), pp. 178 ff.
[23] Thukydides V, 82; cf. also Xenophon, *Hellenika* VII, 1, 43.

they took also the leading part (one of the φυλαί of Thurioi was called 'Αχαΐς[24]). A more precise date might be established if the sanctuary of Zeus Homarios were to be discovered and could be dated. If the Sybaris which allied itself with Kroton and Kaulonia is Sybaris on the Traeis[25] the alliance must be dated not very long after the foundation of Thurioi, since Diodoros relates that the third Sybaris was finally destroyed by the Bruttians not very long after its foundation. There is however also the possibility that "Sybaris" means Thurioi, for Diodoros XII, 11 states that Thurioi made a treaty of friendship with Kroton immediately after its foundation— and at that time Thurioi must still have had the name of Sybaris. In this case the alliance must be dated in a still earlier year.

There is furthermore the story of Apollonios, who relates that the Pythagoreans after having been readmitted to Kroton were killed in a battle against Thurioi. The story is suspect on account of the figure of 60 Pythagoreans which Apollonios seems to have taken from the source of Justinus, who mentions it in a very different connection.[26] Yet we have already shown that Apollonios, though using details found in his sources in a very arbitrary way in order to give more color to his picture, scarcely ever invents anything by himself. In addition, we know of the long war between Thurioi and Tarentum (as we have seen above), and the latter city had been for a long time and was still allied with Rhegion. In this some connection may be found with Iamblichos 250-51, where Aristoxenos tells us that one of the Pythagorean leaders, Archippos, went to Tarentum while the others assembled at

[24] Cf. Diodoros XII, 11.
[25] One might contend that it is not very likely that the Achaeans should have promoted an alliance that included a city founded in opposition to Thurioi, a colony in which they themselves had so large a part. Yet the possibility is not entirely excluded.
[26] Cf. p. 58.

Rhegion and tried to resume their activities there. It is also noticeable that Tarentum remained a stronghold of Pythagorean influence up to the middle of the fourth century when the Pythagoreans had emigrated from all the other cities of Southern Italy. One may, therefore, conjecture that the Pythagoreans, who some time after the great disaster had slowly regained their influence, took some part—if not militarily, at least politically—in the war waged by Tarentum on Thurioi, and that this is reflected in the story of the 60 Pythagoreans told by Apollonios. Yet, with the evidence available at present, this must remain a conjecture.[27]

But let us see how the rest of Aristoxenos' account fits in with the accounts given by Polybios and Apollonios and with our knowledge of the history of Southern Italy in general. The latest event mentioned by him is the final general exodus of the Pythagoreans from Italy. Since, according to Aristoxenos, Archytas at that time was the only one among the leading Pythagoreans to stay, and since his political activities can be traced down to about 360, the exodus can scarcely have occurred much more than about 30 years before that date. This makes it extremely probable that this exodus coincides with the latest event related by Polybios II, 39: namely, the abolition under the pressure of the elder Dionysios of the moderately democratic constitutions which had been created

---

[27] Rostagni (*op. cit.*, pp. 558–560) has tried to reconstruct the history of the Pythagoreans in the second half of the fifth century much more completely by means of synchronisms. But most of them are rather arbitrary. The fact, for instance, that the dispute over the founder of Thurioi was settled through an oracle from Delphi and that the agreement between the Krotonians and the returning Pythagoreans was also favored by the Delphic god can scarcely justify the conclusion that both events must have happened at the same time. There is still less evidence in favor of Rostagni's assumption that the establishment of some kind of military dictatorship in Thurioi, mentioned by Aristotle (*Politika* V, 7, 1807 b, 6 ff.) without date, coincides with the return of the Pythagoreans to Kroton.

under the influence of the Achaeans, an event which we have seen must be dated in 388. But there is very strong additional evidence in favor of this assumption:

(1) It explains easily why Archytas was the only one to stay while most of the others had to flee; for Tarentum never came under the supremacy of Dionysios, while most of the other cities did.

(2) That the Pythagoreans of Metapontum and Tarentum were very hostile to Dionysios and actually promoted strong resistance against his advance at the time when Kroton had not only been weakened—as in 388—but conquered by him, is shown by Neanthes[28] and Polyainos.[29] To stay in any of the cities farther south at a time when these had been either conquered by or become more or less subject to Dionysios would have been utterly impossible for the Pythagorean leaders.

(3) That there was a large emigration of Pythagoreans from Italy at precisely that time is proved by a kind of evidence that, as far as I can see, has been completely overlooked. In about 390–350 the so-called Πυθαγορίσται, Pythagorean adepts of a somewhat less aristocratic type who live in extreme poverty, appear in Attic literature. The earliest example is probably Aischines' dialogue *Telauges*,[30] which, like the other works of this author, must have been written some time between 390 and 375. During the same period and a little later the type becomes very frequent in Attic comedy.[31]

[28] Iambl. 189.

[29] V, 2, ii; cf. also the story of Dionysios' elder brother Leptines, V, 8, ii.

[30] Cf. Heinrich Dittmar, "Aeschines von Sphettos," *Philologische Untersuchungen*, XXI (1912), 213 ff.; K. v. Fritz, "Telauges" in Pauly-Wissowa, V A, 194 f. and *Rheinisches Museum*, LXXXIV (1935), 19 ff. That the fictive time of the dialogue falls earlier and in the lifetime of Sokrates is not at variance with the conclusions drawn above since Aischines wants to contrast the poverty of Sokrates with that of the Pythagoristai and is nowhere afraid of anachronisms.

[31] Cf. Antiphanes in *Comicorum Atticorum Fragmenta*, II, 16 and 67

This makes it certain that the final and general exodus of the Pythagoreans from Italy to which Aristoxenos refers coincides with the latest stage of the developments in that region mentioned by Polybios. It must have happened in the late nineties or the early eighties of the fourth century, most likely some time before 388, since both Aristoxenos and Polybios indicate that the Pythagoreans were not driven out in consequence of a conquest but through political pressure that developed from the general situation; this was probably the threatening advance and the increasing influence of Dionysios.

As to the period between the great catastrophe at Kroton and the final exodus from Italy the accounts given by Polybios and Apollonios (that is, Timaios) on the one side and Aristoxenos on the other do not conflict either. Polybios' account is, of course, much more detailed. There can be scarcely any doubt that this is partly due to the fact that Iamblichos gives only a very short extract from the original work of Aristoxenos, and further confirmation of this assumption will be found later. On the other hand, here as elsewhere Aristoxenos will scarcely have been without bias, and while there is no evidence that either he or his authorities invented anything that was untrue, he may have passed over in silence some details which did not fit in with his general view of the character of the political activities of the Pythagoreans. At any rate the only additional information which his account contains as compared with that of Timaios, the assertion that Rhegion became for some time a centre of the order, is to some extent confirmed by what we know of the general history of that city.[32]

Kock; "Kratinos the Younger," *ibid.*, p. 290; Aristophon, *ibid.*, p. 279; Alexis, *ibid.*, pp. 370 and 377. As to the dates of the first performances of these plays, cf. A. Wilhelm, *Urkunden dramatischer Aufführungen in Athen*, pp. 42, 55 ff., 127.

[32] Cf. p. 74; p. 76, notes 28 and 29.

There remains the problem of Polybios' describing as a general rebellion against the Pythagoreans in Italy what Aristoxenos speaks of as a rebellion in Kroton only; for that both of them refer really to the same event will be proved by the chronology. What Aristoxenos says about Lysis is confirmed by the fact that in the second half of the fifth century Pythagorean influence begins to be felt in central Greece. That one of the centres of Pythagoreanism was in Thebes is borne out by Plato's *Phaedo* with its reference to the Theban Pythagoreans Simmias and Kebes, who are also friends of Sokrates, and to their teacher Philolaos. That Epaminondas was influenced by Pythagorean doctrines can also scarcely be doubted. The date of the birth of Epaminondas is not known. The statement of Plutarch[33] that Epaminondas did not enter public life before he had reached the age of 40 is somewhat vague and may be derived from the notion that Pythagoreans were supposed not to be trusted with higher functions before that age. But considering the part he played in Theban history, he can scarcely have been born much later than between 410 and 405. Plutarch[34] tells us that Lysis died shortly before the Theban exiles who had sworn to liberate their country assembled secretly in Thebes (379). His account is heightened with fictitious additions. But his chronology coincides with what one would have to infer from other considerations. If Lysis was the teacher of Epaminondas he cannot have died earlier than between 390 and 380. All sources, on the other hand, agree that he was already a very old man when he became acquainted with Epaminondas, and that he did not live very long after having become his tutor. Plato's *Phaedo* as well as later sources show that Pythagoreanism must have been flourishing at Thebes for a considerable time when Sokrates died in 399. Aristoxenos tells us that Lysis stayed

[33] *De lat. viv.*, 3, 1129 C.
[34] *De genio Socr.*, 13 f., 583 ff.

CHRONOLOGICAL QUESTIONS 79

for some time in Achaia before going to Thebes. On the basis of this evidence, then, the latest date for his flight from Italy would be about 430. Considering, on the other hand, that he could not have died before 390 or 385, and that he must not only have been an adult but somewhat advanced in Pythagoreanism at the time of his flight, the very earliest date would be about 455. But it seems more likely that the catastrophe happened some years later. This is in perfect harmony with the conclusions drawn from Polybios, Apollonios, and the general historical situation in the middle of the fifth century,[35] according to which the Achaean intervention that followed the Pythagorean troubles must have taken place some time, but not very long, before the outbreak of the Peloponnesian War.

A few additional remarks may be made at this point. Since Aristoxenos[36] mentions several Phliasians among the "last Pythagoreans" and since one of them, Echekrates, lived at Phleius at the time of the death of Sokrates, that is, before the second and complete exodus of the Pythagoreans from Italy, it is extremely likely that Aristoxenos made some mention of these relations in his Βίος Πυθαγόρου. This part of his story is left out in the poor extract from his work in Iamblichos 251. The story told by Plutarch[37] according to which the Italian Pythagoreans lost all trace of Lysis after his flight until Gorgias discovered him by chance at Thebes and brought word of it to Italy is rather suspect. It seems, on the contrary, that there gradually developed a lively intercourse between the Pythagoreans who remained in Italy and their friends in the Greek motherland during the last quarter of the fifth century. It seems that Plutarch's story is a fictional embellishment of the original history. It is also possible that

[35] Cf. p. 73.
[36] Iambl. 251.
[37] *De gen. Socr.*, 13 ff.

Lysis' stay in Achaia had something to do with Achaean mediation in Pythagorean affairs in Italy.

There is still the numismatic evidence to be considered. Kahrstedt[38] has tried to prove by an analysis of so-called Alliance coins that Kroton must have had the supremacy over a large part of the Greek regions in Southern Italy from the time of the destruction of Sybaris until the middle of the fifth century, when it rather suddenly broke down. He linked this event with the Pythagorean disturbances and with the reconstruction of Sybaris in 453. He also tried to arrive at a more precise chronology. Let us briefly consider the evidence.

One regards as Alliance coins different types of coins which show: (1) either the symbol of one city on the obverse and the symbol of another on the reverse, or (2) the initials of two different cities, or (3) both. These Alliance coins are not restricted to Kroton. There are coins of this kind connecting Siris and Pyxos, Sybaris and Poseidonia, Mystia and Hyporon. This shows that a mint system common to two cities was not entirely unusual in Southern Italy in those times. But the Alliance coins of Kroton are much more frequent and comprise many more "allied" towns than those of any other city. This seems to indicate a widespread influence of Kroton, whether economic or political, and all the more so since some of the "allied" cities seem not to have had any special coins exclusively their own during the period of their "alliance," while Kroton always had coins bearing the symbols of Kroton exclusively.

But the material must be examined in somewhat greater detail. The most archaic example is a coin with a tripod of Kroton and ϘPO on the obverse and the bull of Sybaris in incuse on the reverse.[39] Since the Cittanuova hoard,[40] which

---

[38] U. Kahrstedt, *Hermes*, LIII (1918), 180 ff.
[39] E. Babelon, *Traité des monnaies grecques et romaines*, III, Pl. LXX, 11.
[40] Cf. F. von Duhn, *Zeitschrift für Numismatik*, VII, 308 ff.

CHRONOLOGICAL QUESTIONS

is probably to be dated not later than 494, contains not only coins of this incuse type, but also some, though only a few, coins of the later type with both sides in relief, it seems probable that the incuse type was replaced by the relief type at about that time.

Among the incuse coins one can further distinguish between a larger and thinner type which is earlier and a smaller and thicker type which is later. The Kroton-Sybaris coins are neither of the smallest nor of the largest type but somewhat in between. Since the incuse coins begin about the middle of the sixth century, this dates the Kroton-Sybaris coins fairly near the time of the destruction of Sybaris. The question therefore arises whether they were struck before its destruction. In this case they would point to a monetary alliance between the two cities, which would not be impossible since some time before the outbreak of the hostilities that led to the destruction of one of them they had been allied against Siris. Yet one might contend that it would be improbable that the symbol of the more wealthy and more powerful city should be on the reverse. If they were minted after the destruction, there are two possibilities. They indicate either that Sybaris was not completely destroyed (as is related by the historians), part of it remaining as a Krotonian dependency, or that they were made in celebration of the victory.[41] Pending a thorough investigation of all the available material nothing very conclusive can be said about this problem.

There are coins of almost the same style as the Kroton-Sybaris coins with the tripod on the obverse and the bull of Pandosia and ΠΑΝΔΟ on the reverse.[42] In this case the bull is in relief, but within an incuse frame. They cannot be dated much later than the Kroton-Sybaris coins. Since Pandosia

[41] Cf. G. F. Hill, *Historical Greek Coins*, p. 49, note 2; and Grose, *Numismatic Chronicle*, XV (1915), 191.
[42] Babelon, *op. cit.*, III, Pl. LXX, 12 and 13.

had not been destroyed, these coins certainly point to a monetary, if not a political, alliance; and since there are no independent coins of Pandosia of the same period, Kroton seems to have had some kind of supremacy.

Again of almost the same style are certain coins with the tripod on the obverse and the helmet of Temesa in incuse and TE on the reverse.[43] But there are also a good many Kroton-Temesa coins of the later relief type with TE on the side of the tripod and ϘPO on the side of the helmet, that is, with interlaced symbols and names.[44] They belong to the most archaic type of relief coins and can be dated from about 490 to the middle of the fifth century on the basis of our present knowledge.

Of about the same style we have also coins (1) with the tripod of Kroton and the cock of Himera,[45] (2) with the tripod and ϘPO on one side and the Pegasus, which otherwise is the symbol of Korinth, and Ϙ on the other,[46] (3) with the tripod on both sides but the inscription ΚΑΥΛ on one of them.[47] This is the only case in which it is certain that a coin was made for two cities and yet bears the symbol of only one of them on both sides.

This leads to an important special question. There are some coins of about the same style as the ones just mentioned with the tripod on both sides but with the inscription DA on one of them. Kahrstedt considers these coins as evidence of an extension of Krotonian supremacy over Ζάγκλη; and since these coins undoubtedly belong to the fifth century, and the

[43] *Ibid.*, II, 1, p. 1455, No. 2170.
[44] L. Forrer, *Greek Coins: Sicily and Italy* (London, 1922), Vol. I of *The Weber Collection*, Pl. XXXIX, No. 1008.
[45] *Ibid.*, No. 1006.
[46] *Ibid.*, No. 1019; cf. also Grose, *Catalogue of the Fitzwilliam Museum*, I, Pl. LIII, 18 and 19.
[47] Babelon, *op. cit.*, II, 1, p. 1458; cf. also B. V. Head, *Historia Nummorum*, p. 95.

CHRONOLOGICAL QUESTIONS 83

name of Ζάγκλη at that time was restored to Messana for a very short period only following the overthrow of the rule of the sons of Anaxilas in about 460, he has drawn the further conclusion that at that time the influence of Kroton must have reached its greatest extension.

There are two issues of this coin. In one of them[48] the downstroke of the D is prolonged, while in the other it is off the fan so that the downward part may be omitted.[49] This induced Grose to take the first letter as P, which would dispose of Kahrstedt's theory. I do not think it very likely that Grose is right in this respect, since the slope of the letter is much larger than is usual in a P on the coins and the whole letter, if meant to be a P, would be much bigger than the accompanying A, which would also be very unusual. I consider it much more likely that the longer downstroke in one of the issues is due to a fault in the die.[50] But even in this case it is not quite certain that the coin belongs to Zankle; for since there is no symbol on the coin, except the tripod of Kroton, the letters may be the initials of the name of a magistrate, and all the more so, since the side with DA shows a thymiaterion to the right of the tripod, and this is known as one of the insignia of magistrates.

There is one more coin that presents a special problem. This is a coin with the tripod on the obverse and a bull very much like the bull of Sybaris on the reverse.[51] Since both sides are in relief, there can be no doubt that the coin belongs in the fifth century. But it belongs to the most archaic coins

[48] Grose, *op. cit.*, Pl. LIII, 15.
[49] A coin of this issue is in the possession of Mr. E. T. Newell of the American Numismatic Society, who was so kind as to show it to me. The first letter on it is much more like D than like P.
[50] Cf. also the D on the DANK coin in Babelon, *op. cit.*, III, Pl. LXXII, where the downstroke is also a little bit too long.
[51] Grose, *op. cit.*, Pl. XXXVIII, 30; cf. also Grose, *Numismatic Chronicle*, XV (1915), Plate VIII, No. 4.

of this type. Unless it was made under very peculiar circumstances, it can scarcely be dated as late as even the earliest coins of Thurioi-Sybaris,[52] therefore much less probably in the time of Sybaris on the Traeis. Thus it can scarcely represent an alliance between Kroton and this Sybaris. It is not very likely that the Sybaris of 453 which was destroyed by Kroton so soon after its foundation would have had a monetary alliance with this city. Also there are Alliance coins that connect this Sybaris with Poseidonia,[53] and even these coins are less archaic than the Kroton-Sybaris coin. This excludes the probability that this coin may celebrate the second destruction of Sybaris as suggested by Grose.[54] Must it then be considered as conclusive evidence of the existence of some remainder of Sybaris in the first half of the fifth century? There is perhaps still one other possibility, as pointed out by Mrs. Brett in oral discussion. She suggested that the bull on this coin might not be the bull of Sybaris, but that of either Pandosia or Aminaea, since there is no inscription indicating the name of the city. The first part of this suggestion must probably be rejected, since the bull of Pandosia[55] is rather different. But if the ⌐ ᛙ Ⱥ on the coin given by Babelon as number 13 of Plate LXVII[56] means Aminaea, the second part of her suggestion might have to be very seriously considered, since the bull on this coin is very similar to the bull of the coin in question.

As to the rest of the coins listed as Krotonian Alliance coins

[52] *Catalogue of the Fitzwilliam Museum*, I, Pl. XXXVIII, 28 and 29.

[53] *Ibid.*, 24 and 25. The inscription ΣΥ, of which, according to Grose, there are traces on the coin—they are not visible in the photograph—leaves no doubt that the bull on the reverse in this case represents Sybaris, but it is noticeable that the bull has his head turned forward and that No. 25 shows a flying Nike above the bull.

[54] *Numismatic Chronicle*, XV (1915), 191.

[55] Cf. Babelon, *op. cit.*, III, Pl. LXX, 12 and 13.

[56] *Op. cit.*, vol. III.

by Head[57] and mentioned by Kahrstedt,[58] it has not yet been possible to determine the names of the cities or villages that might be indicated by the inscriptions. Since in all the cases that have not yet been discussed in this inquiry there is a tripod on both sides, it must remain an open question as to whether the letters indicate the name of a magistrate of Kroton or the name of an allied city. As our conclusion we may say that at the present stage of our knowledge some of Kahrstedt's more detailed chronological conclusions cannot be accepted as more than mere conjectures; but his evidence is quite sufficient to prove his main point: that Kroton exercised a widespread economic and probably also political influence in Southern Italy towards the end of the sixth and throughout the first half of the fifth century, while the disappearance of Krotonian Alliance coins and the appearance in the second half of this century of independent coins of several cities which up to that time had had their coins in common with Kroton indicates a strong decrease if not a complete breakdown of her power.[59]

It is noticeable that this coincides approximately with the date of the Pythagorean troubles, as determined in our previous inquiry. There can be scarcely any doubt that both events were to some extent interrelated, for the internal troubles of Kroton could scarcely fail to have repercussions on her foreign policy and vice versa. It is natural to assume

[57] *Historia Nummorum*, pp. 95–96.
[58] *Hermes*, LIII (1918), 184.
[59] C. C. Felice, *Archivio storico per la Calabria e la Lucania*, III (1933), 45 ff., has objected to this conclusion on the ground that the "Alliance coins" are partly of a later date. His authority is Head (*op. cit.*, p. 95), who dates the coins 480–420. But Head obviously does not mean to say that the coins cover the whole period from 480 to 420 but that, on the basis of the studies made up to the time when he wrote his book, they had to be dated within this period. This is by no means at variance with Kahrstedt's results.

that the restoration of Sybaris in 453 had also something to do with it. Kahrstedt contends that the restoration would have been impossible unless Kroton had previously been weakened by the Pythagorean disturbances. Rostagni, on the other hand, thinks that the destruction of Sybaris in 448 shows the continuing influence of her archenemies, the Pythagoreans. The flying Nike on one of the coins of the Sybaris of 453[60] might be considered as a $\tau\epsilon\kappa\mu\acute{\eta}\rho\iota\text{o}\nu$ in favor of Kahrstedt's theory, if interpreted as indicating a victory—probably over the hereditary enemy Kroton. But the chronological calculations based on the age of Lysis[61] make it more probable that the catastrophe occurred somewhat later. A final decision is not possible at the present stage of our knowledge, but there can be no doubt that the persecution occurred within the chronological limits indicated above.

The period about which we are least able to arrive at reliable and satisfactory conclusions is that between the first conquest of Sybaris in 510 and the great anti-Pythagorean outbreak in the middle of the fifth century. But it is perhaps possible at least to arrive at an evaluation of the tradition.

We may perhaps start from a special and rather puzzling problem. The chronological investigation has proved beyond any reasonable doubt that Aristoxenos in his account of the burning of the house of Milon refers to the same event as Timaios in his story of the burning of the $\sigma\upsilon\nu\acute{\epsilon}\delta\rho\iota\alpha$ of the Pythagoreans all over Italy. Yet Justinus,[62] whom we have identified with Timaios, says that 60 Pythagoreans perished when their assembly house in Kroton was burnt and dates this event in the lifetime of Pythagoras. How can this be explained? One may, of course, say that in this detail Justinus or Pompeius Trogus followed the version of Dikaiarchos,

[60] Cf. footnote 53 of this chapter.
[61] Cf. pp. 78–79.
[62] XX, 4.

CHRONOLOGICAL QUESTIONS 87

who told the same story. But the evidence against this assumption is extremely strong.[63] We have, then, to assume that Timaios mentioned two rebellions, one in the early part, the other in the middle, of the fifth century. This assumption in itself does not cause any difficulty. For the character of the two rebellions as described by Timaios is entirely different. The first of them is restricted to Kroton, is caused by a common suspicion on account of the secrecy of the meetings of the Pythagoreans, and is not confined to any special political party. The second rebellion, on the other hand, starts spontaneously in a great many different places, and is caused by democratic opposition to the oligarchic policy of the Pythagoreans. But what can be said of the historicity of this account?

In dating the burning of the house of Milon in the lifetime of Pythagoras Timaios agrees with Dikaiarchos. Have we then to accept this verdict of a two to one majority against the story of Aristoxenos, especially since the latter has been proved to be prejudiced in favor of the Pythagoreans? This would be a very rash conclusion. For though Timaios obviously tried to distinguish the character of the two rebellions as described by him there is enough of a duplication of events in his account to make at least one of his stories suspect, and in this case the first of them, since he can scarcely have been completely mistaken about events of the magnitude of those which occurred in the middle of the fifth century, especially since here the history of the whole of Southern Italy was concerned. What is more important, the last Pythagoreans may have had every reason to make the rebellion of the middle of the fifth century appear as restricted as possible, but they can scarcely have committed the gravest errors concerning the one single event in which their revered teacher had been personally involved. For this is the very thing that

[63] Cf. Chapter III.

would be most vividly remembered by a man and by his devoted followers. The error of Timaios and Dikaiarchos, on the other hand—if error it be—can be most easily explained, since Dikaiarchos relied entirely on popular tradition and Timaios also made his inquiries on the spot, but at a time when the "last" Pythagoreans had long been dead.

There was a general tendency, equally strong with ancient authors dealing with the history of philosophy or mathematics and with the historians, to relate everything Pythagorean to Pythagoras himself. There was a remembrance that some struggles had occurred during the lifetime of the master. The great rebellion had started with the burning of the house of Milon, who was known to have been a contemporary of Pythagoras. This fact especially was bound to cause a confusion of the different events in popular tradition though logically there is not the slightest difficulty in the assumption that the burning occurred in a house which was still known as the house of the famous athlete Milon fifty years after his death. It seems therefore that in this detail Dikaiarchos and Timaios are wrong and Aristoxenos is right. This assumption is further confirmed by a very compelling argument that can be drawn from an analysis of Timaios' account itself. For the very extent and violence of the anti-Pythagorean outbreak in the middle of the fifth century as described by Timaios in connection with the general history of that period—it can be inferred to some extent even from the account given by Aristoxenos—make it impossible to accept the story of an earlier revolution amounting to a virtual destruction of the order as told by Justinus and Apollonios. One has only to compare the story of the final exodus of the Pythagoreans in about 390 with the events of the middle of the fifth century to see the difference very clearly.

If this is so, the whole tradition concerning the earlier struggles of the Pythagoreans must be used with very great caution. Dikaiarchos' story of Pythagoras' escape from the burning house, of his flight to Kaulonia and Lokroi, where he is not allowed to stay, of the answer given by the Locrians when he appeals to them for aid—how could any record of this have come down to the fourth century?—and of the refuge he found at last at Metapontum, all this is clearly popular legend and should never have been accepted as serious history.[64] The story of the 300 young Pythagoreans as told by Timaios[65] is likewise suspect since it is connected with the story of the burning of the house of Milon, which as we have seen has been projected back from the middle into the first part of the fifth century.

Yet even the tradition about this part of the history of the Pythagoreans is not quite without value. The story that Pythagoras finally migrated from Kroton to Metapontum and died in the latter city may be true or may merely reflect the fact that Pythagorean influence became strong in Metapontum at an early date. But that Metapontum was one of the first cities after Kroton to come under Pythagorean influence can scarcely be doubted since it is confirmed by the policy of that city and by the fact that Pythagorean reminiscences were very strong there up to a rather late time.

That there had been anti-Pythagorean disturbances long before the great revolution of the middle of the fifth century must also be acknowledged; it is natural, and even Aristoxenos admits as much. The name of Kylon is connected with these early struggles by virtually all the ancient authorities, and this makes it extremely likely that some memory of these events, though interwoven with legends, had survived. But we would serve no useful purpose by trying to analyze all the different legends about Kylon which Iamblichos and Porphyrios found in the works of Nikomachos and Neanthes of

[64] Cf. E. Ciaceri, *Storia della Magna Grecia*, II, 260 ff.
[65] Cf. pp. 56 ff.

Kyzikos. The story of a rift between two groups within the order itself, the ἀκουσματικοί and μαθηματικοί,[66] must also be eliminated from the present investigation since this problem cannot be solved except in connection with an inquiry into the religious and philosophical tenets and the scientific pursuits of the Pythagoreans.

But there is one more question that has to be considered in this connection, that of the tyrant Kleinias, mentioned by Dionysios of Halikarnassos XX, 7.[67] Unfortunately this is the only passage in which this tyrant is mentioned, and we do not know Dionysios' source, nor is he himself one of the most reliable of ancient authors. If Dionysios' story has any historical foundation and if Kleinias is to be dated approximately in the time of Anaxilas—for even this is not certain since we have only an extract from this part of the work of Dionysios— it would illustrate another episode in the prolonged struggle of different political parties for supremacy in the Italian cities of the early fifth century. But the tyranny can scarcely have been more than a transitory episode. For it did not prevent the further spread of Pythagorean influence. It is not recorded in any ancient historical work that has come down to us, except the one passage in Dionysios. And it has found no expression whatever in the coins—if we may judge from the material collected before now—in contrast, for instance, to the tyranny of Anaxilas or to the political changes in Zankle-Messana or in Thurioi, all of which can also be traced in the coinage of these cities.

This must make us cautious not to connect rashly the numismatic evidence for a widespread influence of Kroton in Southern Italy during the first half of the fifth century with the account of Dionysios who tells us that Kleinias succeeded in robbing many towns of their liberty. For what the coins

[66] Cf. pp. 59 ff.
[67] Cf. p. 68.

indicate, while not suggesting any change in the regime at Kroton, extends over a much longer period than the tyranny of Kleinias can possibly have lasted. Nor could the lasting influence of the Pythagoreans be explained if the extension of the power of Kroton had really been due to a tyrant—unless, of course the "tyrant" himself was a Pythagorean like Archytas of Tarentum, who is sometimes given this title. But there is no evidence to support the latter assumption, and anything which goes beyond the rather negative statements made above remains for the time being in the realm of mere speculation.

The few positive results at which we could arrive in regard to this period can be summarized very briefly. There is no doubt that there were anti-Pythagorean movements in the early part of the fifth century, but these movements must have been of an entirely different character from those of the middle of that century. There must have been other political struggles and changes in Kroton as well, perhaps even including the transitory establishment of a tyranny. But none of these events obviously prevented the gradual spread and intensification of Pythagorean influence in Southern Italy.

Still less can be said about the first establishment of the Pythagorean order as a religious and political society on Italian soil and about its first activities. The lasting enmity between the Pythagoreans and Sybaris as well as the character of the earliest Alliance coins, which can scarcely be dated later than about 500, indicates that the order must have played some part in politics as far back as the destruction of Sybaris in 510. Therefore of all the dates given by ancient authors as to Pythagoras' arrival in Italy that of Timaios, 529,[68] obviously comes nearest to the truth. But we do not know from what kind of evidence he derived this date nor how accurate it is. If the symbol of the tripod on the coins of Kroton could

[68] Cf. p. 55.

be explained as indicating the influence of the "Apollo religion" of the Pythagoreans, Pythagoras' arrival would have to be dated in a still earlier time, since some of the coins of this type are unquestionably older than 530. But we know much too little about these things to be able to draw such a conclusion.

There are, of course, a great many stories about Pythagoras' political activities, his dealings with Telys, the "tyrant" of Sybaris, and the like; but though the person of Telys is undoubtedly historical, the stories connecting him with Pythagoras are conflicting and obviously legendary so that it would be futile to discuss them here in detail. Here again we have to content ourselves with the few facts that can be ascertained.

As a result of this part of our investigation we may list the following dates:

(1) The arrival of Pythagoras in Kroton and the foundation of the order c. 530 B.C.

(2) An early anti-Pythagorean movement in Kroton in the beginning of the fifth century: the rebellion of Kylon. This movement did not prevent the further extension and intensification of Pythagorean influence over a period of approximately forty years.

(3) The great anti-Pythagorean outbreak, including the burning of the house of Milon at Kroton, between 450 and 440 B.C. This led to the first emigration of Pythagoreans from Italy and the establishment of Pythagorean centres at Phleius and Thebes. Those Pythagoreans who had not emigrated gradually regained some political influence by adopting to some extent the democratic principles which they had formerly opposed. Rhegion became probably for some time the centre of their activities.

(4) The final exodus of the Pythagoreans from Italy (except Archytas and his friends in Tarentum) c. 390. Appearance of the Πυθαγορίσται in the Greek motherland.

From future investigations we may expect with some confidence a solution of several problems: Excavations at Sybaris ought to show whether a Sybaris existed in the time between the destruction of the city in 510 and its restoration in 453. A thorough examination of all the relevant points by numismatists may: (1) solve the problem of whether the DA coin and the coins with OP, IA, YΛI, ME, etc.,[69] are Alliance coins or not, and (2) make it possible to determine more exactly the date of the different monetary alliances, and consequently of the rise and fall of Krotonian influence and power. Discovery of the sanctuary of Zeus Homarios may provide us with some hints as to the date and the character of the confederacy of Kroton, Kaulonia, and Sybaris. That there will also be some new evidence concerning the earlier period of the political history of the Pythagorean order cannot be said with as much confidence.

[69] Head, *op. cit.*, pp. 95–96, and Kahrstedt, *op. cit.*, p. 184.

CHAPTER V

The Character of the "Pythagorean Rule"
In Southern Italy

ᛐᛐᛐ

THERE remains the question of the character of the Pythagorean "rule" or influence in Southern Italy and of possible changes in the character of this influence. Unless very unusual discoveries should be made, it is not very likely that future excavations or numismatic studies will contribute very much to the solution of this problem. But fortunately it seems possible on the basis of the evidence in our possession to arrive at somewhat more definite conclusions in this respect than in regard to chronological details.

Here again we must start from the period about which we have somewhat more reliable and detailed information: the period from the middle of the fifth to the beginning of the fourth century.

We have seen that in spite of the attempt made by Aristoxenos or by his authorities to obscure the fact it is evident from his account as well as from that of Timaios that the anti-Pythagorean revolution in the middle of the fifth century was a widespread movement extending over virtually all the more important Greek cities in Southern Italy with the exception of Tarentum.

This seems to presuppose that the "rule" of the Pythagoreans also extended far beyond the boundaries of Kroton, since otherwise there would be no point in so widespread a revolution against it. All the ancient authorities, furthermore, including Aristoxenos, agree that the order was strictly organized and centralized. Yet there is no trace whatever of a centralized government comprising even so much as Kroton and Metapontum, the main seats of Pythagoreanism in the early fifth century, much less Tarentum and Rhegion, which at different times within this period also came under strong Pythagorean influence.

This difficulty has been much discussed, and has led either to the assumption that the "rule" of the order was confined to Kroton, and consequently that the tradition about "revolts" in other cities as well is wrong, since there can be no revolution without a rule against which it is directed—but all the evidence is against this assumption—or to an exaggerated conception of the importance and extent of Krotonian supremacy in the first half of the fifth century.

But there is a third possibility, which, it seems to me, gives the solution of the problem. Ancient tradition does not provide the slightest evidence for the existence of anything like a real rule of the Pythagoreans in any of the cities of Southern Italy at any time.[1] But all the authors agree that they tried to bring about a moral regeneration on the basis of their philosophical tenets and religious beliefs first in Kroton and later in other cities in which they acquired influence, that on some occasions they had a decisive influence on the course of foreign policy (for instance, in regard to the relations between Kroton and Sybaris, and later between Dionysios the elder and Tarentum), and that they took sides in the struggle between aristocratic and democratic tendencies in the middle of the fifth century. They also indicate that many individual Pythagoreans were at different times members of the govern-

[1] See Appendix C.

ment in their cities. But this is very different from a rule of the order as such.

Analogies are always misleading if taken literally, but they sometimes serve to illustrate a point if considered in the right perspective. In the present case, if one looks for a historical analogy, one may find a parallel in the history of Freemasonry of the 18th century. The doctrines, of course, are entirely different, but there is a certain analogy in the fact that in the 18th century a great many leading men in all fields—statesmen, philosophers, poets, composers—were Freemasons, just as in the fifth century many Greek leaders in Southern Italy were Pythagoreans. The attitude of these Freemasons, their views, and their actions were influenced by Masonic ideas in varying degrees. Yet they certainly did not govern, compose, or write poetry in their quality as Masons, much less because they were Masons. The unity of the Pythagorean order, its organization, its hold on its members, was probably much stronger than that of the Masonic society, especially during the first period of its history. A Pythagorean statesman would in all likelihood be much more Pythagorean in his actions than Frederick the Great was ever Masonic, but none of them, on the other hand, was ever so absolute a ruler as this king.

Yet the parallel may serve to illustrate the following point. If in the 18th century there had been a general persecution of the Freemasons in Europe, a very great number of leading men would have disappeared from public life and the political consequences would have been very great. Yet none of them would have been a ruler, a statesman, or a political ruler because he was a Mason. This is exactly what Polybios, Apollonios, and Aristoxenos suggest in the case of the persecutions of the Pythagoreans.

Since only very short extracts of the works of Aristoxenos and Timaios have come down to us, we find no detailed evidence showing that this interpretation of their accounts is right. But it is confirmed by the fact that the kind of Pythagorean "rule" which we postulated for the fifth century continued in the fourth century wherever Pythagorean influence survived. Archytas, for instance, was *strategos* and the leading statesman at Tarentum for many years during the second quarter of that century and he had a strong influence at least on the foreign if not on the internal policy of other cities as well. His political principles were strongly influenced by Pythagoreanism. Yet he certainly was not *strategos* because he was a Pythagorean and because the Pythagoreans ruled his city, but he was freely elected under constitutional procedure. If the policy of his city became "Pythagorean" it was so because he personally adhered to Pythagorean principles.

In this respect, then, the character of the Pythagorean "rule" seems to have remained the same from the time of Pythagoras himself to the final disappearance of the order. This, however, does not exclude the possibility or probability that there were also very considerable changes. In the later part of their history the Pythagoreans seem always to have adhered to an extremely conservative policy. When the old aristocratic principles had to struggle against the new democratic principles the Pythagorean order was the stronghold of aristocraticism. When the established democracies had to fight against tyranny the Pythagoreans came out strongly in favor of democracy. This conservativism seems to have been inherent in Pythagorean doctrine since they always favored order and strict moral principles. Yet there must have been a time when they were newcomers and when consequently what was new in their doctrines must have come in conflict with accepted notions and traditions. The struggles which developed as a result of this situation must have been of an entirely different character from those which occurred when the Pythagoreans had become more or less identified with an established regime. This is in perfect harmony with what remains of Timaios' account after subtraction has been made of those elements of his story which really belong in the history of the revolution of 450–40.[2] It is most likely that in those early times in spite of the hierarchic tendencies of the order the strongest opposition came from those among the aristocrats who looked upon themselves as the preservers of the old traditions. Another cause of resentment may have been that aristocratic birth was not considered sufficient to entitle a man to admission to the order. This is exactly what the oldest versions of the Kylon story imply, and this story, as we have seen, is the one which is most likely to contain some, however obscured, reminiscences of this early period. It is only Apollonios who mixes this story with an account of the struggles between aristocrats and democrats in the middle of the fifth century.

The acceptance of the general outline of this part of the Kylon story as historical truth is not at all at variance with the fact that the Pythagoreans later became identified with the aristocratic party. For it is natural—and there are many examples in recent history—that a political party when it is on the decline will gladly accept the support of, or conclude an alliance with, a political group which it would have despised and fought—and which it often actually has fought—at the time of its power. The Pythagorean order with its hierarchic tendencies was admirably fitted to become a supporter of aristocratic government in the time of rising democratic tendencies. But it is also quite understandable that the Pythagoreans at a time when the struggle between oligarchy and democracy had been superseded by new developments could gradually regain some of their influence and finally became sincere supporters of the rather conservative democracies of the late fifth and the early fourth century, especially

[2] Cf. pp. 86 ff and 89 f.

in their struggle against the extension of the rule of the conquering tyrant Dionysios, whose political principles must have run much more strongly counter to the convictions of the Pythagoreans than those of a conservative democracy. This shows that the "last Pythagoreans" were not quite insincere in the interpretation they gave to Aristoxenos of the political history of their order in the early fifth century though this interpretation was historically not quite adequate either.[3]

This much then can be said about changes in the internal policy of the Pythagoreans. But it seems that there were also some changes in the way in which they conducted their foreign policy. They obviously started by creating strongly organized societies under very strict rules first in Kroton,[4] then in other cities as well. These societies tried to acquire political influence and seem to have taken a strong hand in active politics as far back as the great struggle between Kroton and her mighty neighbor Sybaris in 510. The success of such a policy would then naturally have increased the influence of the Pythagoreans in other cities, while this in turn must have made it easier for Kroton, the centre of their activities, to acquire a leading position in Southern Italy without being compelled always to have recourse to the methods of power politics. In spite of the setbacks which the Pythagoreans suffered from political opposition in Kroton itself they were able gradually to build up a complicated system of international policy which included very friendly relations with some cities, alliances with others, and a kind of supremacy over the smaller towns nearest to Kroton; but—disregarding the possibility of a transitory tyranny at Kroton—they did not try to establish outright domination anywhere, as is indicated by the fact that even the very small towns were allowed to put their own name on the coins which they had in common with Kroton.

[3] Cf. pp. 30–32.
[4] Cf. Appendix C.

In its general outline this seems to have been the method of Pythagorean policy up to the time of Archytas. Yet one can observe that there were also considerable changes, necessitated by a change in the general political situation. All the ancient authorities agree—and their view is confirmed by all sorts of independent evidence—that in the earliest period the order was very strictly organized and that everything was directed from one centre. In the second period—after the revolution of c. 450—the Pythagoreans, we are told, again tried to create a centre of their activities, this time at Rhegion. But if we look at the single instances of their activities, it does not seem that they succeeded in again creating a strictly centralized organization. What we can observe is rather a free collaboration of the different groups that managed to survive and to recover some political influence in various of the Southern Italian cities.

In the time of Archytas the situation had changed again. There is no evidence that at that time any considerable Pythagorean groups survived in any of the cities except in Tarentum. If, therefore, the traditional Pythagorean policy of alliances proved so successful when applied by Archytas it was due, not to collaboration of Pythagorean groups in different cities, but to the fact that this policy was particularly suited to the general political situation as it had developed at that period.

This attempt to analyze the changes in Pythagorean policy from the end of the sixth to the middle of the fourth century is, of course, partly speculative. But the development which I have tried to trace seems to be logical, and the view of its different phases is at least supported by a considerable amount of historical evidence.

One more remark may perhaps be made, in the hope of throwing some light on another problem. There is a striking resemblance between the form of Pythagorean "rule" and the way in which Plato and the Academy later tried to take part in active politics. Erastos and Koriskos at Assos, Hermias at Atarneus, Dion in Syracuse, etc. did not become political leaders as members of the Academy. Erastos and Koriskos were elected magistrates under a democratic constitution. Hermias had been a tyrant long before he became acquainted with Platonic doctrines and gave his people more freedom in consequence of his becoming an admirer of Plato. The attempts of Plato and Dion to convert the younger Dionysios to Platonic principles reminds us strangely of the story of how Pythagoras persuaded Simichos, the tyrant of Kentoripe,[5] to lay down his rule voluntarily and to establish a government in harmony with Pythagorean principles, but not under Pythagorean rule. And though Dion's struggle for power at a later time was partly motivated by the desire to put Platonic political ideas into practice, even he did not become a ruler in his quality as a Platonic philosopher, much less as a member of the Academy, but in the course of the development of the political situation at Syracuse.

This similarity must not be interpreted as due to Pythagorean influence on Plato—though in view of his own testimony in the seventh letter one would be mistaken to deny such influence altogether. As in other cases—in pure philosophy one may compare the affinity of some of Plato's later doctrines to those of the Eleatics—he arrived in the course of his own development at principles similar to those of other philosophers, and it was this natural affinity rather that made him susceptible to their influence.

If this has not always been acknowledged, it is due to the

[5] The Simichos story may, of course, be a later invention. But it will scarcely be possible to defend the opinion that Timaios' version of the history of the Pythagoreans, which is confirmed by such various kinds of independent evidence, is based on the inventions of later Platonists and Pythagoreans.

fact that Plato's "originality" has been regarded as sacrosanct by many Platonists and as something from which no detraction is ever allowed. But the originality of a genius does not consist in the fact that every detail of his thought or method is completely new—this is a rather inferior type of originality, though rather common in our times—but in the depth and penetration of his thought, and in the fact that every detail in his thought, though not always absolutely new in itself, comes to bear his imprint.

APPENDIX A

The Emendation of Iamblichos' Passage, οἱ δὲ λοιποὶ κτλ.[1]

A. ROSTAGNI[2] has objected to Rohde's emendation because he thinks that the meeting at Rhegion was only a phase in the emigration of the Pythagoreans from Italy, so that the order of the words is not to be changed, but a lacuna must be assumed following προβαινόντων. His view has been accepted by L. Deubner in his recent edition of Iamblichos' *Vita Pythagorae* (Teubner, 1937). But Rostagni's explanation does not solve the difficulty. In his opinion the seemingly contradictory statement that the Pythagoreans left Italy and assembled at Rhegion is but an awkward expression and really means that they met there on their way into exile. However, if one accepts this explanation and consequently leaves the order of the words unchanged, the whole sentence οἱ δὲ λοιποὶ τῶν Πυθαγορείων ἀπέστησαν τῆς Ἰταλίας π λ ὴ ν Ἀ ρ χ ύ τ ο υ τ ο ῦ Τ α ρ α ν τ ί ν ο υ refers to the time of the Krotonian catastrophe. This would imply that at that time Archytas was an adult and a man of some consequence. On the other hand, the author says that Lysis was a young man when the disaster occurred. Lysis died as an extremely old man (as we have seen, p. 87) when Epaminondas was scarcely more than a boy; that

[1] See p. 13, footnote 17.
[2] *Atti della R. Accademia delle scienze di Torino*, XLIX (1914), 564, note 4.

is, between 385 and 380 at the very latest. Consequently Archytas, who was head of the government of Tarentum in 362 and probably for some time after, cannot have been an adult, much less a man of political consequence at a time when Lysis was a young man. This cannot have escaped the notice of the author of the passage, who seems rather well informed about this part of his story. Hence it is impossible that the sentence οἱ δὲ λοιποὶ κτλ. originally referred to the time of the disaster at Kroton. The transposition of words proposed by Rohde is therefore absolutely necessary.

There still remains the question of whether we have to assume a lacuna preceding the words ἦσαν δὲ οἱ σπουδαιότατοι.... Rohde thought it necessary to make this assumption, and all scholars since, including Rostagni, have accepted this view. There is, however, perhaps some confusion in the argument. There can be little doubt that Aristoxenos must have said something about the fate of the "last Pythagoreans"—his personal acquaintances—in the period after they had left Italy. But it is by no means necessary to suppose that this part of his account was taken over into the extract made from his work by Nikomachos or some other author. So there is no real reason to assume a lacuna in the text of the manuscripts, though the original must have contained more than what we now read in Iamblichos. There is also a chronological problem involved which we discuss elsewhere (pp. 75 f.).

APPENDIX B

Iamblichos' Contradictory Statements in Sections 248–251[1]

IAMBLICHOS' carelessness is so great that it is impossible to make out with certainty how his contradictory statements originated. But the following observations may be made:
1. Archippos and Lysis, who are mentioned in Iamblichos 250, recur in the same connection in a quotation from Neanthes in Porphyrios 55. This makes it all the more likely that this part of the passage Iamblichos 248–251 is derived from Aristoxenos (as we have seen, pp. 15 ff.), since Aristoxenos, as shown above (p. 16) is Neanthes' main authority. 2. Corssen[2] has drawn attention to the fact that the way Aristoxenos is quoted in Iamblichos 252 (ταῦτα μὲν οὖν 'Αριστόξενος διηγεῖται) is very similar to the way Nikomachos usually quotes him.[3] This makes it very likely that not only the passage Iamblichos 252, for which Nikomachos is cited, but also the Aristoxenos citation in Sections 248–251 is derived from him. 3. The view attributed to Nikomachos in Iamblichos 252 is exactly the same as that of οἱ μὲν in the Neanthes passage

---
[1] See p. 14, footnote 19.
[2] Pages 340 ff.; see p. 3, footnote 1.
[3] Porph. 61: καὶ ταῦτα μὲν 'Αριστόξενος ἀπήγγειλε; Iambl. 237: καὶ ταῦτα μὲν 'Αριστόξενός φησι.

APPENDIX

in Porphyrios 54. This makes it almost certain that Nikomachos made use of the work of Neanthes. For Iamblichos cannot have committed the error of citing Nikomachos instead of Neanthes, since Neanthes did not share the view of οἱ μέν (as we have seen, p. 10). But if Nikomachos quoted from Neanthes, he can scarcely have quoted the view of Neanthes' οἱ μέν without mentioning also the contrary opinion supported by Neanthes himself. How, then, are we to account for the fact that Iamblichos attributes their view to Nikomachos without restriction?

The most plausible explanation, in my opinion, is the following. Iamblichos, as usual, had read his authority very superficially. He found that most of the versions quoted by Nikomachos—all those, in fact, of which he (Iamblichos) had so far taken notice—agreed in the statement that Pythagoras was not present when the disaster at Kroton occurred. So he made a general statement to this effect in his introduction. Then he copied the extract from the work of Aristoxenos which he found in Nikomachos. Having done this he discovered to his surprise that Nikomachos referred also to a version which was at variance with the general statement that he (Iamblichos) had made in his introduction. Hence he omitted this version and quoted a third version mentioned by Nikomachos (that of Neanthes' οἱ μέν) under Nikomachos' name, without being aware that the adversative particle with which it was introduced in the work of Nikomachos had become meaningless.

This explanation, which otherwise might appear improbable, must be considered in the light of the following facts: 1. Iamblichos in his quotations from other authors has not infrequently left out a sentence without which the context is unintelligible. Thus the ἀλλ' in this sentence from Iamblichos 30: πλείονες ἢ δισχίλιοι τοῖς λόγοις ἐνεσχέθησαν, ἀ λ λ ' ὁμοῦ σὺν παισὶ καὶ γυναιξὶ ὁμακόειον ἱδρυσάμενοι . . . παρέμειναν

APPENDIX

ὁμονοοῦντες is as unintelligible as the μέν in the Nikomachos quotation in Section 252, until one reads the same passage in Porphyrios 20, where it runs like this: πλέον ἢ δισχιλίους (sc. αὐτὸν) ἑλεῖν τοῖς λόγοις ο ὖ s μ η κ έ τ ' ο ἴ κ α δ ' ἀ π ο σ τ ῆ ν α ι, ἀ λ λ ' ὁμοῦ σὺν παισὶ καὶ γυναιξὶ ὁμακοΐον παμμέγεθες ἰδρυσαμένους . . . κτλ. 2. Iamblichos very frequently replaces a quotation by name by an impersonal quotation and vice versa.[4]

[4] Cf. Iambl. 30: ὥs φασι and Porph. 20: ὥs φησι Νικόμαχος or Iambl. τεκμήραιτο ἄν τις and Porph. 59: τεκμαιρόμεθα δέ φησι Νικόμαχος.

APPENDIX C

Interpretation of an Apollonian Sentence in Iamblichos 252

THE SENTENCE of Apollonios in Iamblichos 252: Ἔπειτα καὶ τῶν νεανίσκων ὄντων ἐκ τῶν ἐν τοῖς ἀξιώμασι καὶ ταῖς οὐσίαις προεχόντων, συνέβαινε προαγούσης τῆς ἡλικίας μὴ μόνον αὐτοὺς ἐν τοῖς ἰδίοις οἴκοις πρωτεύειν, ἀ λ λ ὰ κ α ὶ κ ο ι ν ῇ τ ὴ ν π ό λ ι ν ο ἰ κ ο ν ο μ ε ῖ ν, if read superficially, might seem to be at variance with a statement above.[1] But what does this sentence really imply? Certainly not that the νεανίσκοι actually ruled the city and that they did so in their quality as Pythagoreans. On the contrary: as the following words, μεγάλην μὲν ἑταιρείαν συναγηοχότας, show, they are supposed to have formed a political club or perhaps even a political party, which became very influential because it was strictly organized and because many of its members belonged to the leading families of the city. This makes it quite clear that their "rule" is considered by Apollonios, that is, in this case, Timaios, as an indirect rather than as a direct one. This is also expressed by a statement of Diogenes Laertios which is obviously derived from the same source: [οἱ νεανίαι] πρὸς τοὺς τριακοσίους ὄντες ᾠκονόμουν τὰ πολιτικὰ ὥστε σ χ ε δ ὸ ν ἀριστοκρατίαν εἶναι.

[1] See p. 95, footnote 1.

GENERAL INDEX

Academy, and the Platonists, 101
Achaeans, mediation in Pythagorean affairs, 55, 63, 73, 79, 80; institutions and influence, 72, 73, 76
Adcock, F. E., 70n
Aischines, *Telauges*, 76
Alexis, 77n
Alkimachos, 58
Alliance coins, v, 80-86, 93; defined, 80; of Kroton and other cities, 80 ff., 90, 91, 99; incuse and relief types, 81; disappearance of, 85
American Numismatic Society, vii, 83n
Anaxilas, 68, 90; sons, 83
Anaximander, 48
Androkydes, 45, 60
Antiphanes, 76n
Apollodoros, 49; "canon" of, 18, 25
Apollonios of Tyana, 96, 98; fragments of the Timean version obtained by authors from, viii, 34 ff.; tendencies in treatment of authorities, 54, 55, 57, 74; reconstruction of chronology of, 55 ff., 72 ff.; predilection for large-scale historical pictures reason for confused story, 61, 64; coincidence between Polybios and, 63 ff.; account of period between catastrophe and the exodus from Italy, 77 ff.; interpretation of sentence by, in Iamblichos 252, 108
"Apollo religion," 92
Archeological evidence, vi
Archippos, 4, 12, 13, 74, 105
Archytas of Tarentum, 15, 23, 28, 75, 76, 91, 92, 97, 100, 103, 104; story about Kleinias and, 22
Aristophanes, 62
Aristophon, 77 n

Aristotle, 26, 28, 75n
Aristoxenos, 94, 95, 96, 99, 104; reconstruction of versions of Dikaiarchos and, viii, 3 ff.; when used through medium of Neanthes and Nikomachos, viii, 18, 20, 21, 104, 105; share in the later tradition on the political history of the Pythagoreans, 3; survey of fragments that can be attributed to, and of influence on later authors, 5-26; tendency to represent Pythagoras as a bringer of freedom and peace, 16, 20, 24; one of most important authors on life of Pythagoras, 19n; minimizes effect of Kylonian rebellion, 20; traces of, in work of Diodoros, 22-26; four works dealing with Pythagoreanism, 22n; Spintharos, father of, 22, 23, 28, 33; identification of the primary sources from which his knowledge was derived, 27-29, 66; reliability of the different parts of his account, 29-32; how account fits in with those by Polybios and Apollonios, 74 ff.; account of period between catastrophe and the exodus from Italy, 77 ff.; prejudiced in favor of Pythagoreans, 77, 87; versions by, compared with other writers, 86 ff.; citation in Sections 248-51 of Iamblichos, 105
Arnobius, 32
Athenagoras, 32

Babelon, E., 80n, 81n, 82n, 83n, 84n
Beloch, Julius, 56, 70n
Bertermann, W., 3n, 45, 47, 48, 55, 60n, 65
Brett, Mrs. Alexander Baldwin, vii, 84
Busolt, Georg, 70n

GENERAL INDEX

Charondas, laws of, 18, 20
Ciaceri, E., 70n, 89n
Cittanuova hoard, 80
Coins, Pythagorean activities traced through, v, 70 f., 80–86, 90, 91, 93, 99; of Kroton, v, 80 ff., 91, 99; of Sybaris, 70, 81 ff.; of Pandosia, 81
Corssen, F., 3–16 *passim*, 105

Damon-Phintias story, 21, 23, 25
Dareios the Great, 62
Dates, methods of determining, 25 f., 29n, 75n
Deimachos, 57, 58; *see also* Deinarchos
Deinarchos, 57; *see also* Deimachos
Delatte, A., vii, 3n, 6, 7, 27, 32, 33n, 45, 46, 47, 48, 49, 55, 56, 58, 64, 65
Delos, chronology of Pythagoras' stay at, 6, 8, 10, 17, 26
Delphic oracle, 75n
Demokedes, 58, 61, 62
Deubner, L., 103
Dikaiarchos, reconstruction of versions of Aristoxenos and, viii, 3 ff.; age compared with that of Neanthes, 6; popular tradition represented by, 30, 31 f., 88; reliability, 32; value as supplementary source, 32; versions by, compared with other authors, 86 ff.
Diodoros, traces of work of Aristoxenos in, 22–26; influenced by Timaios? 26n; references to history of cities, 28, 68 f., 71 f., 74; extracts from Timaios in works of, 33 ff.; handling of sources, 34
Diogenes, Antonius, fragments obtained by authors from, 18, 34 ff.
Diogenes Laertios, 108; share of Neanthes in accounts given in biography of Pythagoras, vii, 3 ff.; paralleled passages, 9, 36, 37, 39, 44; mention of the last Pythagoreans known by Aristoxenos, 21, 27; allusions in later authors traced to, 32
Dion, 101
Dionysios the elder, 73, 75, 76, 76n, 77, 95, 99
Dionysios the younger, 21, 24, 25, 101
Dionysios of Halikarnassos, 68, 90
Dittmar, Heinrich, 76n
Duhn, F. von, 80n

Echekrates, 27, 28, 79
Eleatics, the, 101
Empedokles, 49, 51n
Enmann, A., 42
Epaminondas, 4, 13, 15n, 28, 65, 78, 103
Erastos, 101

Favorinus, 36
Felice, C. C., 85n
Firmicus Maternus, 32
Forrer, L., 82n
Frederick the Great, 96
Freemasonry, analogy between Pythagoreanism and, 96
Fritz, K. v., 76n
Furtwaengler, A., 70n

Gela, peace conference, 73
Gorgias, 79
Grose, S. W., 70n, 81n, 83, 84

Head, B. V., 82n, 85, 93n
Herakleides Pontikos, 7
Hermias, 101
Hermodamas, 17
Herodotos, 71
Hieron and his brother, 68
Hill, G. F., 81n
Hippasos, 59, 61, 62
Hippolytos, 32

Iamblichos, 28, 74, 77, 89; share of Neanthes in accounts given in biography of Pythagoras, vii, 3 ff.; carelessness and errors, 14, 19, 20n, 57, 105, 106; incapable of making up a coherent story, 16; allusions in later authors traced to, 32, 79; sections of work of, attributed to Timaios, 33 ff.; paralleled passages, 36–40, 43, 44, 53; emendation of a passage in, 103–4; contradictory statements in Sections 248–251, 105–7; interpretation of an Apollonian sentence in, 108

Jacoby, F., 6n
Justinus (identified with Pompeius Trogus), 34, 74, 86; extracts from Timaios in works of, 33 ff.; handling of sources, 34; paralleled passages, 36–38, 40, 43, 44

GENERAL INDEX

Kahrstedt, U., v, 80, 82, 83, 85, 86, 90*n*
Kallimachos, 23
Kaulonia, city, 72, 73, 74, 93
Kebes, 78
Keyes, Clinton W., viii
Kleanthes, *see* Neanthes of Kyzikos
Kleinias, date of reign, 68, 90
Kleinias-Archytas story, 22
Kleinias-Proros story, 23
Koriskos, 101
Kothe, A., 33*n*, 47, 48, 50, 55
Kratinos the Younger, 77*n*
Kreophylos, 17
Kroton, numismatic evidence for supremacy of, v, 80–86, 90, 91, 99; burning of house of Milon, 4 (*see also* Milon); absence of Pythagoras during the disaster, 4, 11, 14, 49, 106; regenerated by Pythagoras' teaching, 18, 50, 51; dating of the disaster, 30, 62 ff., 77, 86 ff., 103 f.; defeated by Locrians, 45, 50; Timean references to, 47; relations with Sybaris, 47, 50, 56, 95, 99; great names at, 61; historical facts, 68 ff., 80 ff.; end of influence, 73, 93; references to rebellion in, and to general rebellion, the same? 78, 87; arrival of Pythagoras, 92; anti-Pythagorean movement dated, 92; a main seat of Pythagoreanism, 95, 99; organized societies in, 99, 108
Kylon, seeks admission to Pythagorean order, 3, 11; rebellion against it, 4, 11, 16, 31, 60, 89, 92, 98; character, 16; dated, 62, 64; many legends about, 89

Leptines, 76*n*
Litages, 57; *see also* Theages
Literary tradition, importance of, vi f.
Lysis, 15*n*, 28 f., 30, 65, 69, 78, 79, 80, 86, 103, 105; escape from fire, 4, 12; death, 13, 79

Macrobius, paralleled passage, 38
Maiandrios, 54*n*
Metapontum, excavations at, v; Pythagoreans in, 76, 89, 95
Meton, 58
Mewaldt, J., 3*n*, 20, 22
Milon, burning of the house of, 4, 12, 86 ff. *passim*, 92 (*see also* Kroton); passage on training of, 8

Neanthes of Kyzikos, share in accounts given by other writers in biographies by Pythogoras, vii, 3 ff., 89; Aristoxenos used through medium of, viii, 105; identity and date of the elder, 6; quotes sources literally, 34; shows Pythagorean hostility to Dionysios, 76; use of, by Nikomachos, 106
Newell, E. T., 83*n*
Nikomachos, 60, 61, 89; Aristoxenos used through medium of, viii, 18, 20, 21, 104, 105; quotes sources literally, 34; view attributed to, in Iamblichos 25*z*, 105; made use of work of Neanthes, 106
Ninon, 56, 58, 62
Numismatic evidence, *see* Coins

Origen, 32

Pandosia, coins, 81
Pantognotos, 53
Phaedo, 27, 78
Phaedrus, 35*n*, 39
Phaidon, 28
Pherekydes, 4, 6, 17, 26
Philolaos, 78
Phintias-Damon story, 21, 23, 25
Pindar, 68*n*
Plato, 23, 28, 101 f.; *See also Phaedo and Phaedrus*
Platonism, viii, 101
Plutarch, 78, 79
Polyainos, 76
Polybios, 72 ff., 96; extracts from Timaios in works of, 33 ff.; handling of sources, 34; coincidence between Apollonios and, 63 ff.; account of period between catastrophe and the exodus from Italy, 77 ff.
Polykrates of Samos, 17, 24, 26, 53, 61, 62
Polyzelos and Hieron, 68
Porphyrios, 30*n*, 89; share of Neanthes in accounts given in biography of Pythagoras, vii, 3 ff., 105; paralleled passages, 9, 36, 43; allusions in later authors traced to, 32; sections of work of, attributed to Timaios, 33 ff.
Poros-Kleinias story, 23
Pythagoras, biographies of, 3; denies

GENERAL INDEX

Pythagoras (*Continued*)
Kylon's request for admission to order, 4, 11; present during tragedy at Kroton? 4, 11, 14, 49, 106; chronology of stay at Delos, 6, 8, 10, 17, 26; death, 11, 48, 55, 89; represented as bringer of freedom and peace, 16, 20, 21; migrations, 17, 25, 48 ff., 89; reason for migration to Italy, 17, 24 f.; fame, 18; widespread influence, 18, 19, 21; regenerating effect of teaching of, 18, 50, 51; Krotonian disaster dated after death of, 30; chronology from nineteenth year to death, 47 ff.; age, 48, 50; head of order in Italy for 39 years, 48; failure or success in Samos? two versions, 51 ff.; introduces Egyptian method of teaching through symbols, 51; brothers, 53; tendency of authors to relate everything Pythagorean to, 88; story of flight from burning house a popular legend, 89; date of arrival in Italy, 91; date of arrival in Kroton, 92; *see also* Pythagoreans

Pythagoras the younger, 51, 52

Pythagoreanism, importance of the literary tradition, vi f.; interrelations between Platonism and, viii, 101; Aristoxenos' four works dealing with, 22*n*; analogy between Freemasonry and, 96

Pythagoreans, problem of the history of their political activities, v–ix; Aristoxenos' and Dikaiarchos' share in the later tradition on political history of, viii, 3 ff.; how the doctrine was preserved, 4; Kylon's rebellion against, 4, 11, 16, 31, 60, 89, 92, 98; Krotonian disaster, 4, 11, 12, 30, 62 f., 77, 86 ff., 103 ff.; history of, from last years of Pythagoras to dissolution of the order, 11 ff.; hope that cities will come to aid of, 12, 16, 25, 30; seek political influence? 16; represented as lovers of freedom and liberal government, 16, 21, 24; "the last," 21, 27–30, 79, 99, 104; friendships, 24; three periods in political history, 29; whether revolution against 30; and its character and extent, 31, 72, 78, 86 ff., 92, 94; connection with Sybaris, 31*n*, 46, 56, 91; Achaean mediation in affairs of, 55, 63, 73, 79, 80; numbers, 56, 57 f., 74, 86, 89; part in struggle between aristocratic and democratic forces, 58, 60, 95, 97–99; split in order as cause of political conflict, 59, 90; great names among, 61; take part in war against Thurioi? 74 f.; exodus from Italy, 75 ff., 88, 92, 103; the Pythagoristai of Attic literature, 76; influence, 78, 89, 90, 91, 92, 108; period between first conquest of Sybaris and great outbreak against, 86 ff; first establishment as religious and political society in Italy, 91; foundation of order, 92; conflicting stories about political activities of, 92; character of the "rule" or influence of, 94–102, 108; foreign policy, 95, 99 f.; cities that were main seats of, 95; *see also* Krotonians

Rhegion, city, 13, 73, 74, 75, 77, 92, 103; strong Pythagorean influence in, 95, 100

Rohde, E., 3*n*, 13, 15, 33*n*, 41, 58, 103, 104

Rostagni, A., vii, 26, 33*n*, 45, 46, 47, 48, 51*n*, 55, 58, 62*n*, 65, 75*n*, 86, 103, 104

Schwartz, E., 22

Simichos of Kentoripe, 18, 101

Simmias, 78

Sokrates, 28, 76*n*, 78, 79

Spintharos, 22, 23, 28, 33

Stobaios, 62*n*

Strabo, 72*n*; story in, and its source, 53 f., 55*n*, 60

Suidas Lexicon, 32

Sybaris, excavations at, v, 92; rule of, 31*n*; Pythagorean relations with, 31*n*, 46, 56, 91; historical facts, 31*n*, 46, 50, 56, 68 ff., 80 ff., 93; relations with Kroton, 47, 50, 56, 95, 99; coins, 70, 81 ff.; period between first conquest of, and great anti-Pythagorean outbreak, 86 ff.; *see also* Thurioi

Syloson, 53

Synchronisms *vs.* dates in establishing chronology, 29*n*, 75*n*

Synkellos, 48

GENERAL INDEX

Tannery, P., 59
Tarentum, 72, 74, 75, 76, 94, 95, 100, 104; under strong Pythagorean influence, 95, 97
Telauges, 76
Telys of Sybaris, 31n, 92
Thales, 48
Theages, 57, 62; *see also* Litages
Thebes, 78, 79
Themistios, 32
Theophrastos, 26
Thukydides, 73n
Thurioi, founded, 63, 69, 73; historical facts, 63, 68 ff.; coins, 84; *see also* Sybaris
Timaios of Tauromenium, 94, 96, 98, 101n, 108; reconstruction of version of, and reliability of his accounts, vii, viii, 33–67; Diodoros influenced by? 26n; importance of work, 32; tradition found in other authors attributed to, 33; lack of facts pertaining to political history of Pythagoreans, 34; very few fragments from, quoted by name, 34, 35; authors through whose works Timean fragments are known, 34 f., 77; reasons for reliability of, 35, 65, 66, 88, 101n; paralleled passages, 36–39; reconstruction of his chronology, 47 ff.; broad historical view, 56, 60, 65, 66, 67; versions by, compared with other writers, 86 ff.
Traeis, city on the, 69; *see also* Sybaris
Trogus, Pompeius, 34, 86; *see also* Justinus
Tzetzes, 48

Unger, G. F., 3n, 73

Wilhelm, A., 77n

Xenophanes, 17
Xenophon, 73n

Zaleukos, laws of, 18, 20
Zankle, coins, 83, 90
Zeus Homarios, sanctuary of, 72, 74, 93